HAMLYN
CREATIVE CRAFTS

MAKING & FLYING KITES

Wolfgang Schimmelpfennig

HAMLYN

Contents

Acknowledgements
Front cover photograph: B.A.C. kite by André Casagnes, photographed by Gill Bloom, Ilford, Essex.
Photographs: Studio G.P. Reichelt
Line drawings: Bernhard Mass

First published 1988 by
The Hamlyn Publishing Group Limited,
Michelin House,
81 Fulham Road,
London SW3 6RB

First impression 1988

Copyright © Falken-Verlag GmbH
Niedernhausen/Ts. West Germany

Copyright © 1988 English translation
The Hamlyn Publishing Group Limited

ISBN 0 600 55895 9

Typeset by J&L Composition Ltd, Filey, North Yorkshire
Printed by Mandarin Offset in Hong Kong.

HAMLYN
CREATIVE CRAFTS

MAKING &
FLYING KITES

Introduction

Kiting has recently become enormously popular, with special clubs and festivals being set up to cater for the thousands of enthusiasts. But kiting is not a new phenomenon, for it has fascinated makers, fliers and spectators alike for over 2,400 years. In defying gravity the kite is a symbol of freedom and independence. With incomparable aerodynamics it uses the wind to hover in the sky as if weightless, only the gentle hum of the string (or line) betraying the battle for supremacy taking place between the forces of lift and gravity.

The Chinese were the first to use kites for military, religious and mystical reasons, with the practice later spreading to other East Asian countries. In Asia, the kite has retained its traditional role in play and sport, while in the West it has also been used for scientific experiments up to and including manned flight.

The attraction today lies in making and flying kites, combined with the opportunities for unbridled creativity, play and sport. The sight of a kite flying high above you unleashes a feeling of freedom, and ever since the first flat kite was invented in Europe in the 15th century it has lost none of its popularity. Furthermore, new materials now make it possible to construct far more complex kites where the emphasis is on producing a smooth flight, one of the most important considerations for the do-it-yourself kite maker.

With the exception of the hexagonal kite train, all models presented in this book have been built and flown by me. The selection ranges over flat kites, box kites and flexible kites to the increasingly popular steerable models, whose pilots can exhibit their expertise in championship contests, and the always exciting kite trains.

The author with a double-Eddy flaero train

The History of the Kite

Although it is difficult to unravel the history of the kite because of the many legends and theories handed down from generation to generation, we do know that the kite originated in Asia. It was then, as it still is today, over 2,000 years later, intricately bound up with religion and mythology. For example, Balinese Hindus believe that kite flying was one of the favourite hobbies of their gods. Consequently, even now no great competition kite undertakes its maiden flight in Bali without first being consecrated by a priest in an elaborate ceremony.

China is generally accepted as being the home of the kite. It is believed that the first wooden kite, in the shape of a bird, was flown there as early as 400 B.C. At this time the kite was used for strategic purposes (for signalling or transmitting news). A well-known Chinese story describes how General Han Hsin was besieging a palace in 196 B.C. He used a kite to measure the distance between his troops and the walls of the palace, and then built a tunnel enabling his troops to get into the grounds undetected and capture the enemy. (Since paper had not been invented at that time kites were made of cloth. Also, it is safe to assume that these early kites were already capable of being manned and were equipped with whizzers, or hummers, for frightening the enemy.)

Shortly after the kite's appearance in China it spread right across the world, with the exception of the Americas, via the trade routes of the time.

1. Korea and Japan c. 700 A.D.   2. Malaysia, Indonesia and the Pacific region c. 2,000 years ago.   3. Via India to North Africa c. 1,500 years ago.   4 To Europe in the Middle Ages. Dotted line indicates possible influence on Europe from Mongolia or via North Africa.

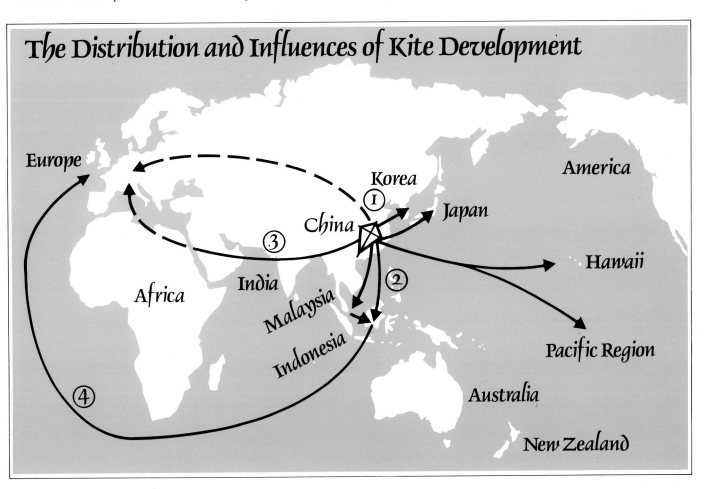

The Distribution and Influences of Kite Development

Korea and Japan

Although kites came to Korea from China there were independent developments there too. One amusing tale describes how General Gim Yu-Sin, who lived in the 7th century, was ordered to quash a rebellion. But one night his soldiers saw a star falling from the heavens which they interpreted as a bad omen signalling the death of their queen. To raise morale amongst his troops General Gim Yu-Sin made a kite which he used to shoot a fireball into the sky. His warriors were completely deceived and believed the star had risen again. Their courage returned and they defeated the rebels.

Traditionally, Koreans build only rectangular fighting kites with a hole in the middle. They are made of bamboo and paper. Since this type of kite is particularly versatile, it is excellently suited to all kinds of kite games which date back as far as the 7th century. The kite competitions always take place in the first two weeks of the lunar year, with people flying kites at the end of these festivals bearing the slogan: 'May all the cares of the last year fly away with this kite'.

In Japanese history the first mention of the kite is in 713. True to its Chinese origins it was used for transmitting news. Initially, however, only wealthy Samurais could afford to build kites from paper because it was very expensive. But later, with the help of new techniques such as wood-printing, the kite became more popular. Ever since, Japanese kites have been decorated with elaborate colourful motifs. Further developments saw the kites being used to lift people in and out of difficult circumstances, such as wars and sieges. In the troubled war years of the 15th and 16th centuries the kite became less important but it later regained its popularity. Today, there are 87 historic kiting centres across the country, including the city of Nigata and its environs. At the beginning of the 18th century kite flying became popular in Shirone, Sanjo and Imamachi, where kite competitions have been held ever since. These competitions have their origins in the power struggles between the great landowners, who owned rice fields on

Wau Bulan from Malaysia

both sides of the rivers. Traditionally, these competitions are fought using the *c.* 3 m/3¼ yd large Rokkaku-dako, or the enormous O-dako. The kites are flown above the river with each team attempting to sever its opponents' kite strings. This 200-year-old spectacle had a beneficial side effect: the poorly fortified river banks were liable to be swept away by heavy rain unless they were strengthened by the hefty stamping of feet by the teams flying their kites.

Malaysia and Indonesia

Kites were probably introduced to Malaysia on their journey from China to Indonesia. Those first flown by the coastal inhabitants were fish kites, made of palm leaves. These kites were flown in Indonesia and the Pacific archipelago and were used, equipped with a line and hook, for catching fish.

Kite flying competitions have been held in Malaysia since the 15th century. Unlike Japan, where the aim is to sever the opponents' strings, points are scored for decoration, flight performance and the highest altitude.

The Eddy kite, familiar all over Europe, has a close relative in the Malaysian bow kite. This type of kite has been flown in Malaysia and Indonesia for many centuries. Kite flying usually takes place during the time of the north-east monsoon on the harvested rice fields. However, today's most popular Malaysian kite is the Wau Bulan, which is mainly manufactured in the north-easterly province of Kelantan.

For centuries kite flying has been a mass sport in Indonesia. The Javanese bow kite is also related to the Eddy kite, and reached Europe via the Portuguese, English and Dutch trade routes.

A variant of the Japanese fighting kite has been widely found in the Indonesian islands for centuries. I have never seen so many kites flying anywhere as on the island of Bali, where, regardless of time and season, they are flown over the rice fields and through even the narrow alleyways of the villages.

Kite flying on Bali has a long practical tradition. The rice farmers fly large kites, resembling birds of prey, over their fields to protect the rice from insatiable swarms of sparrows. The making of kites on this island is tightly bound up with the Hindu faith. The basic motifs on many kites are taken from the story of the Ramayana, with its tales of gods, kings and kidnapped princesses.

This large kite c. 8 m/8¾ yd, with its traditional decoration, is used in Bali's annual 'Lomba Layang Layang' kiting competition

Thailand

The sport of kite flying has been practised in Thailand for over 700 years. In 1358 the kings of the Sukhothai period so enjoyed kite flying that they neglected their official duties, resulting in an edict forbidding the flying of kites in the palace or its environs. However, kites were not flown in Thailand only for sport. As early as the 17th century Thais used them as transporters, sending cargo-laden kites flying over their golden cities. King Petraja even used kites to carry bombs on military operations. He had barrels of gunpowder fastened to kites and exploded them over rebel fortresses forcing many conspirators to capitulate.

At the beginning of the 18th century King Rama II popularised kite flying as a sport throughout the whole country. Ever since, when the south-west monsoon blows, kite competitions are held before the walls of his royal palace. The competition involves several male fighting kites (papkao) trying to sever the string of a large, pentagonal female kite (chula).

Another kite tradition involves flying kites at the start of the north-east monsoon. The kites are meant to persuade the rising winds to drive off the rain clouds and so guarantee a rich harvest in sunny weather.

Europe

As there are no reliable sources for the invention of the kite in Europe it is assumed that it was 'imported' by European seafarers. The history of European kiting begins with the flying of wind socks. As early as the Roman Empire soldiers would attach these kite-like, air-filled pennants to poles in order to frighten off the enemy. Also, fire-spitting kites were used for military purposes in Europe and Asia up to and beyond the Middle Ages.

Since the step from an air-filled pennant to a flying kite is not great, it is not surprising that the first well-known illustration of a European kite (1326) shows a wind sock replete with wings. Probably the most famous sketch of a flying kite appears in a book, *Bellifontis*, by Konrad Kyeser, published at the beginning of the 15th century. The illustration shows a free-flying kite with windlass, string and a schematically presented bridle.

The invention of the flat pennant kite occurred in the 15th century. But while the kite had originally been rectangular with broad tails, by the middle of the 17th century it was joined by curved and rhomboid models.

In his study of the history of kite making, *Kites An Historical Survey*, Clive Hart discusses the fact that until the start of the 18th century the kite had not played a significant part in the development of air travel. In contrast to Asiatic countries, where kiting was a standard feature of sporting events, the kite in Europe remained no more than a plaything for adults and children.

However, towards the middle of the 18th century the kite became more popular. In France in 1736 it even reached the point where there were riots between opposing teams of kite fliers, resulting in the banning of kiting in public places. Sixteen years later Benjamin Franklin made an important scientific discovery. He flew kites during gathering storms to prove that the electric charge in the clouds is identical to the electrical charge produced by friction in a glass sphere. The electrical force of the lightning striking his diamond-shaped kites was conducted to earth via the line. It was strong enough to set alcohol alight and was used for performing other experiments.

In the following years members of the 'Franklin Kite Club', founded in Philadelphia, used kites for making electrical and meteorological readings. Until then balloons used for this purpose had been frequently forced aground by the strong winds and could not be used to measure wind speed.

Experimental successes with kites made it possible to build the first models capable of transporting people in the first third of the 19th century. In 1825 the Englishman George Pocock developed a kite that could fly his adult daughter up to 100 m/109¼ yd off the ground. Later, he devised systems of kite-drawn carriages which were used over the country roads of southern England. These carriages were capable of transporting four or five people at speeds of up to 30 kmph/18½ mph. One of the advantages was that there were no road tolls for these kite-drawn carriages.

The kite was also used to ferry ashore victims of shipwrecks when, in 1861, Sir George Nares developed a dirigible (or steerable) kite. Since the coastline was nearly always to the lee side of the shipwreck (sail boats would be forced towards the shore by the wind, where they would be stranded) kites could be used successfully. Experiments with man-carrying kites were also conducted in Germany during the First and Second World Wars when they were sent up to improve the limited chances of spotting enemy submarines.

At the turn of the century, the American born Samuel Franklin Cody (who lived in England where he earned his living in a Wild West Show) carried out many experiments with kites. His main interest, too, was in using the kite to transport people. After a long series of experiments he developed the box kite (also called the bat because of its wings).

In Cody's 'Man lifting system' it was not an enormous kite that produced the pull required to lift a human being, but rather a train of several box kites functioning as a sort of anchor in the sky at a height of some 800 m/875 yd. The number of these pulling kites depended on the wind speed. A two-winged kite served as the transporting kite, which was attached to a system of pullies on the main line. A basket with room for one person hung below the pulley systems. By manipulating various strings the pilot could sufficiently alter the kite's angle of incline to effect ascent and descent along the main line.

Berlin's Alfons Czech with his perfect copy of a Cody

Multicelled tetrahedral invented by Alexander Graham Bell

Cody patented his kite system in 1901, and then began to engage the interest of the English admiralty in its military applications. He showed them the enormous pulling power of his system in 1903, when he crossed the Channel in a boat drawn by kites.

Meanwhile, in many European countries, people were experimenting with powerful kites which were also capable of transporting people. Other kites were used to set up altitude records, with competitions being the only means of deciding which kite could fly highest. The most famous constructors of that period were the Englishman B.F.S. Baden Powell (11 m/12 yd giant kite) and Charles Brogden (angled-surfaced winged kite), the Frenchmen Sacconey and Madiot (box kites) and the Russian officers Schreiben and Ulyanin. A kite that is still particularly popular today was invented by the American William A. Eddy. His Eddy bow kite was developed in 1891 and was later used for taking meteorological readings at particularly high altitudes. Since his childhood, Eddy's main interest was in hexagonal kites and, from 1887, he began an intensive study aiming to construct a tail-less kite capable of stabilising itself. The result, his Eddy bow kite, was the first genuine step forward in the development of kite making since the invention of the rhomboid kite in the Middle Ages.

Although Eddy knew of the existence of the Javanese bow kite his model was an independent development. It had no tail and the keel formed by the central cross-spar ensured its stability. Through his invention other kite makers became aware of the bow kite, resulting in more models.

Incidentally, Eddy had some curious experiences as a kite designer. People wondered why a grown man was flying kites. One day a boy came up to him and said, 'My father says you should have someone keeping an eye on you', but the scoffer had to change his mind when Eddy's doctor friend also began to get involved in kiting. At roughly the same time, Alexander Graham Bell (the inventor of the telephone, then living in America) also began experimenting with a diverse series of kites.

Like many other kite makers of the time, Bell too had the idea of building a flying machine capable of carrying people.

In order to cover large distances by kite it had to be equipped with a motor and propeller. Probably Bell's most remarkable invention was the tetrahedral kite which is still flown by many kite makers today. And in 1907 he created a 3,393 celled tetrahedral. This giant silk-covered kite, equipped with floats, had to be towed behind a steam boat on Baddock Bay, Nova Scotia, Canada. On its maiden flight in December 1907 it flew for seven minutes at a height of 60 m/65½ yd before it crashed and broke into pieces. Bell also constructed a large number of successful model kites which, without doubt, brought manned flight one step nearer.

Lawrence Hargrave, born in England in 1850, was another kite inventor whose work did much for the development of aviation at the turn of the century. He studied aerodynamics and began to take an interest in kites in 1880. His early works concentrated on inventing a flying machine capable of flying cross-wind, similar to the way sailboats do. But when Hargrave had no

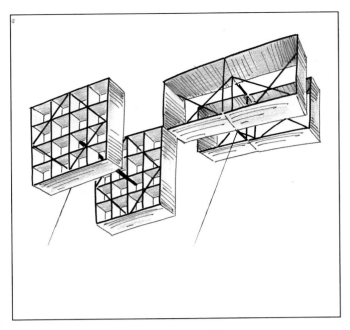

Box kites by L. Hargrave (1850–1893)

A Hawaiian train

practical success he turned his attention to kite flying. He experimented with a multitude of models until he invented his Hargrave box kite in 1893. The advantage of his box kite was that it has a large sail surface area within a relatively small space. The vertical sails between the aerofoils stabilise the kite, relinquishing the need for a tail.

Hargrave took the development of the kite forward a second time by equipping his box kite with curved aerofoils. It was known that aerofoils with a curved wing section could develop greater uplift than a flat one.

Hargrave's box kite became the standard model for meteorological readings in the following years.

After the Second World War it was the American aeronautical engineer Francis Rogallo whose inventive spirit and innovatory ideas brought forth a new type of kite. In order to be independent of the wind and weather during his experiments he installed a ventilator with a 1.5 m/1¾ yd radius in his house. Aiming to construct a kite that would develop maximum lift from minimum sail area he designed a kite with flexible wings and aerofoils. Unlike kites with rigid aerofoils this type could adapt to the wind and so ensure effective lift.

Rogallo patented his flexible kite, which later became the basis for many other types of kite. Even the American dirigible kite, the Hawaiian, is based on the principle of flexible aerofoils. Like Rogallo, the American D.C. Jalbert started from the assumption that the form of the kite must keep step with changing wind movements. Initially, Jalbert experimented with a series of box kites before he invented the parafoil in 1965. The parafoil easily gets airborn, with the wind filling up its cells. The carrying elements are curved fabric profiles between two sails.

A kite festival

Materials

Tools

Any handyman with a basic tool set will be adequately equipped to make the kites in this book. Here is a list of the tools illustrated below.
1. Scissors
2. Soldering iron with a fine head for cutting and joining ripstop nylon
3. Knife for sharpening wood and bamboo strips
4. Stanley knife
5. Pencil sharpener for sharpening the ends of wooden sticks
6. File for deburring and scoring
7. Saw for cutting and nicking
8. Hammer
9. Folding rule
10. Ruler
11. Punching tongs for punching holes in material or pipes
12. Riveting tongs (or pliers)
13. Pencil
14. Lighter for melting together the ends of nylon string
15. Cutting pliers
16. Iron for smoothing out sail material (not illustrated)
Good tools are essential for successful kite making. It is particularly important to have sharp scissors for cutting ripstop nylon (the scissors should be used exclusively for this purpose).

Fabrics

The material used for covering the kite plays a decisive role in whether it will fly successfully or not. Its wind resistance and weight will determine both stability and flight behaviour.
1. *Pergamyn* (kite paper)
   Kites have been covered in this material since time immemorial. The advantages include being easy to glue and its light weight. Particularly vulnerable spots can be strengthened by gluing on several layers. The disadvantage of pergamyn is that it rips easily, particularly in wet and humid conditions.
2. *Tyvek*
   This material, made of polyethylene, is similar to paper and is often used in kite making. It is characterised by high resistance to tear and low weight. Normally, tyvek is held together using a cellulose tape, but it can also be machine-sewn

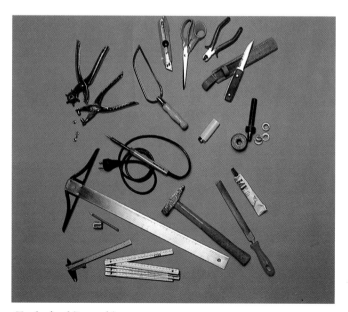

Tools for kite making

The covering materials described above

without difficulty. Tyvek can be painted with water-base hobby paints, and is available from kite shops and hobby shops.

3. *Ripstop nylon*
Recently ripstop nylon has become more popular for covering kites. The material is available in various grades and has an extremely high tear resistance. The somewhat cumbersome problems of working it on a sewing machine are compensated by its high loading capacity. Ripstop nylon is available from sail makers and kite shops; the cost varies depending on quality.

Notes
1. In the UK dowelling comes in *diameters* of 6 mm/ ¼ in, 8 mm/⁵⁄₁₆ in, 10 mm/⅜ in, and 12 mm/½ in. When using the diagrams alter the diameters to one of these measurements.
2. Pergamyn is similar to parchment or craft paper.
3. Flying line is sold by breaking strength in the UK, not by line diameter.

Frames

The choice of frame material determines the weight and rigidity of the kite, and therefore its flight efficiency. Whilst most kites manage with a wooden or bamboo frame, dirigible kites should have frames made of fibre glass reinforced synthetics.

Ramin wood and beech dowelling, available in specialist shops, are suitable for kite making. It is worth noting that ramin wood is more flexible than beech wood, and its frame is therefore more likely to take on a dihedral shape under wind pressure than one made from beech wood. Since this distortion is undesirable in box kites, select beech wood.

Bamboo rods are particularly suited for making kites because their high rigidity means that they can be used even in high winds. Many Asian kites are made of split bamboo rods, which are astonishingly supple and very strong. Bamboo rods are available from timber merchants or kite shops.

Due to its relatively light weight, aluminium is occasionally used as a frame material. There are various alloys available (for aeroplanes and arrow shafts) which combine remarkable lightness with great rigidity.

In recent years, modern materials have become increasingly fashionable in kite making, most of them coming from ship or aeroplane construction. Fibre glass reinforced synthetics are popular for dirigible kites, and are available from kite shops either in tube or rod form with diameters of 2 mm/¹⁄₁₀ in upwards. But since fibre glass is heavier than wood such kites need more wind. Also note that care must be taken when working fibre glass synthetics because inhaling the fine shavings can damage your health.

Carbon fibre tuning has proven to be a particularly high grade material for kite making. The tubes are extremely light yet very rigid. Carbon fibre tuning comes into its own in kites where there is a particular need for wing twisting rigidity. Carbon fibre rods are often used for fast dirigible or facet kites. Fibre glass fishing rod tubing is also used. Its advantages are that it is light, and its cone-shaped ends give way under wind pressure.

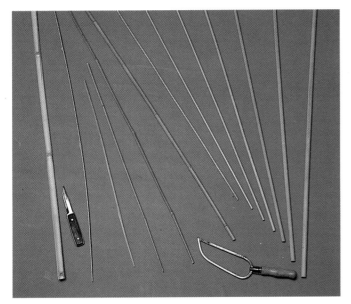

Dowel and bamboo rods

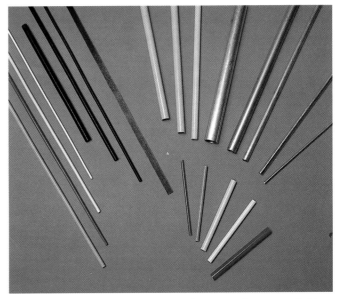

Fibre glass and carbon fibre rods of various diameters; fishing rod blanks of various sizes and aluminium piping

Kite Strings and Swivels

The choice of the right kite string requires careful consideration. Breaking strength, stretch, and wind resistance all need to be borne in mind. The synthetics used in today's kite strings, such as nylon, perlon, trevira and aramid, are relatively damp proof. Even so, there is no sense in allowing the kite string to get unnecessarily wet.

To avoid being caught out you should ensure that the breaking strength of the string is at least twice as great as the anticipated wind speed (drag). As the drag is variable you can use different strings on different days.

Carbon fibre lines of the same breaking strength as nylon lines have a considerably smaller diameter. The lower air resistance and lighter weight of these aramid lines are advantageous in kite flying. The disadvantage is that the thin wires cut into your skin when reeling in, making the wearing of leather gloves a must.

Finally, never knot the string or tail directly onto the bridle, always use a swivel with a carabiner (or snap) whose strength should also be measured against the drag on the kite.

Jointing Materials and Accessories

The construction elements and parts shown here are essential for kite flying. They are generally available from kite shops, and also from hobby and angling shops, chandlers, and specialist shops for technical equipment.

Injection moulded rigid synthetics, such as cross joints, T, Y or L joints, are indispensable to the kite maker. You can, however, make the parts yourself using rigid synthetics such as nylon block. Aluminium V-joints are quickly produced but do lose their form in stronger winds.

PVC and fibre glass pressure tubing are important aids for making T, cross and L joints. Using rubber O-rings allows you to make cross joints that can be dismantled again. Arrow nocks can be used to secure bows and rings. They are attached to the ends of the tube with an aluminium connector or are fixed to the ends of sharpened wood. Use swivels and carabiners to secure the string to the kite. Parts of the sails or frame can be tensed using a line tensioner. Metal O and D joints are jointing elements between the sails and frame. Carabiners are attached to the eyelets in the sail. Capping the ends of the spars protects against injury and prevent the sail from being torn.

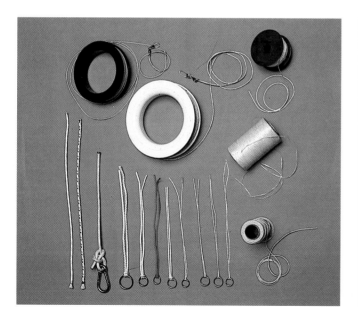

A variety of swivels, with snaps and kite lines of various strengths and materials

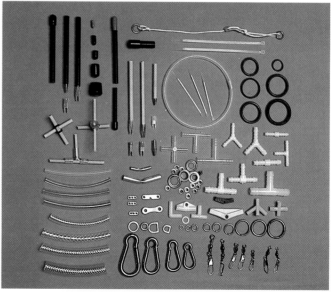

Jointing materials and other accessories

Knots

Knots are every bit as indispensable to the kite enthusiast as the string itself. Being able to tie them is part and parcel of the pilot's flying and safety skills. A knot should hold and give when it has served its purpose.

The knots and hitches presented here are the product of a thousand year's seafaring experience. They can also be used in the making and flying of kites.

1. Toggle hitch – for securing the kite string to a rail (acute angled drag).
2. Round turn with two half hitches – for securing the kite string to a rail (angle of drag c. 90°).
3. Clove hitch – see round turn with two half hitches.
4. Double sheet bend – used to join two unequally thick ends. It can be tied with a single or double hitch.
5. Reef knot – used to join ends of equal thickness.
6. Figure of eight – used to prevent the line slipping.
7. Rolling hitch – used to tether the line to a secure object.
8. Securing a bow to a ring, reel or carabiner.
9. Half blood knot – non-slip bows at the end of the line. Used for securing strings to rings, lashings or eyelets.

If you practise tying these knots and hitches then you will not be in the embarrassing position of having to tie a granny knot in future.

Working with Bamboo

Asiatic kites are traditionally made of strong but highly flexible bamboo. The Japanese fighting kite, the Malaysian Wau Bulan and the Balinese Janggaan are three examples. Take care when buying bamboo to ensure that it has been aged (dried), otherwise it may split at room temperature. Also, since bamboo from certain regions (Indonesia, for example) may be infested with insects it is advisable to treat the bamboo with insect spray before use to prevent it cracking later.

Bamboo rods of a few millimetres diameter are now available and can be used for making kites from 1 m/ 3¼ ft upwards. The spar of an Eddy kite should be constructed from two bamboo parts. An aluminium tube joins the parts leaving the thinner tips of the bamboo pointing outwards. In the case of the spine, the thicker end should be at the rear edge of the kite.

Splitting bamboo is less problematic than it might seem. The bamboo rod, which must be at least 2 cm/¾ in thick, is cut twice crosswise. Use a strong knife for the cutting. To keep the edges parallel you need to apply gentle pressure at the nodes. These quarter parts are then finely split using a narrower blade. Split bamboo rods can be bent over steam or a flame. The fine splinters that are produced when splitting bamboo penetrate the skin both very easily and deeply. You should take great care when working with this material and remove splinters with a file.

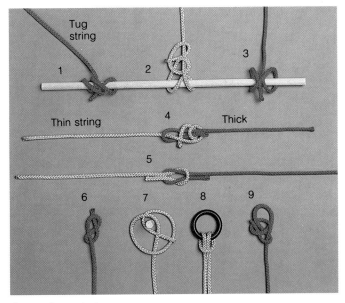

See main text above.

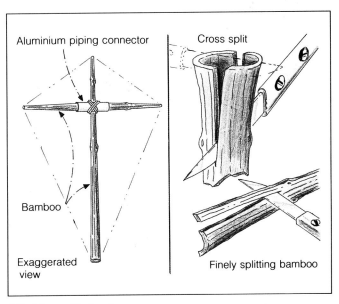

Working with bamboo

Sewing Techniques

Modern tear resistant textiles are being increasingly used in kite making. Tyvek is usually held together with a synthetic adhesive, but can also be sewn. Use a polyester twine of 60–70 strength. As tyvek will not slip on the sewing machine it is easy to sew.

Ripstop nylon, available in various weights (20–65 g/ ¾–2¼ oz), is more difficult to work due to its silicone coating. Polyester twine of 50–70 strength and Jersey needles (size 11) are suitable for sewing nylon fabrics. Test the various seams and hems on a practice piece first before sewing the kite sail.

The best way to start is by fixing the seams in position with pins or adhesive. The tension on the upper and lower threads of the machine must be adjusted exactly to match the nylon being sewn. If necessary, have an expert set the tension for you. For perfect stitching you must be careful how you feed through the material. Professional sailmakers have machines with a rubber roller behind the machine which feeds the nylon through it. For making kites, sewing machines fitted with a 'soft transport' are best, which have rubber surfaces to feed through the material.

To ensure perfect feeding when using ripstop nylon, the material should be pulled *gently* through the machine with the left hand. Ripstop nylon is usually cut using a hot soldering iron which allows the material to be joined at the same time, requiring only the seam to be sewn. A double seam is more resilient and looks perfect.

Seams are sewn using a straight stitch (2–3 mm/¹⁄₁₀ in stitch lengths).

The various hems and seams are illustrated in the fold out on the back page. Seams are sewn with a straight stitch or zigzag stitch. Do not make the stitches too close together or the fabric will become perforated. The strongest seam for joining two pieces of fabric is the lap seam (see sewing techniques). The first seam can be glued together. Seams that are particularly exposed to pressure can be sewn using the stretch stitch.

Reinforcements made of dacron, webbing or seam binding are essential when sewing kite sails. If these materials are sewn on to the sail it is usually necessary to adjust the tension on the threads and to use thicker needles.

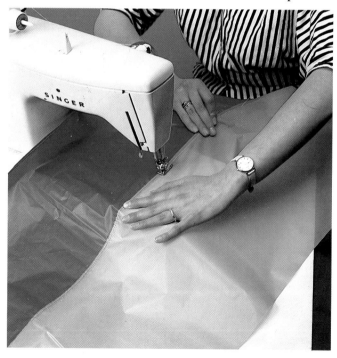

Sewing ripstop nylon

A variety of webbings and seaming tapes, dacron and thread

Making Colourful Kites

One of the main reasons for the steadily increasing number of kiting enthusiasts stems from the marvellous opportunities for making colourful kite sails. You can be as imaginative as you like, producing fine, exhillerating displays.

Tyvek can be painted with water-based paints with no problem at all. First draw your design in pencil, and then colour in the shapes with paint. An existing motif can be projected on to the tyvek from a colour slide.

Ripstop nylon can also be decorated with water-based emulsion paint or silk paints. However, instead of painting the ripstop nylon combine different coloured nylon fabrics for much bolder colour effects. Draw the outline of the sails on a piece of paper and gradually build up the pattern. The pieces of fabric are then cut out and sewn together.

Another way of decorating the sails is to apply pieces of fabric to the cut sail. Design the pattern on paper first, before the individual sections are transferred on to the material and cut out with a soldering iron. Fix the nylon pieces to the sail using pins or a synthetic adhesive. Sew the pieces to the sail using a zigzag stitch and remove the excess material with a soldering iron.

Painting tyvek

A colourful Peter Powell train

Making Kites

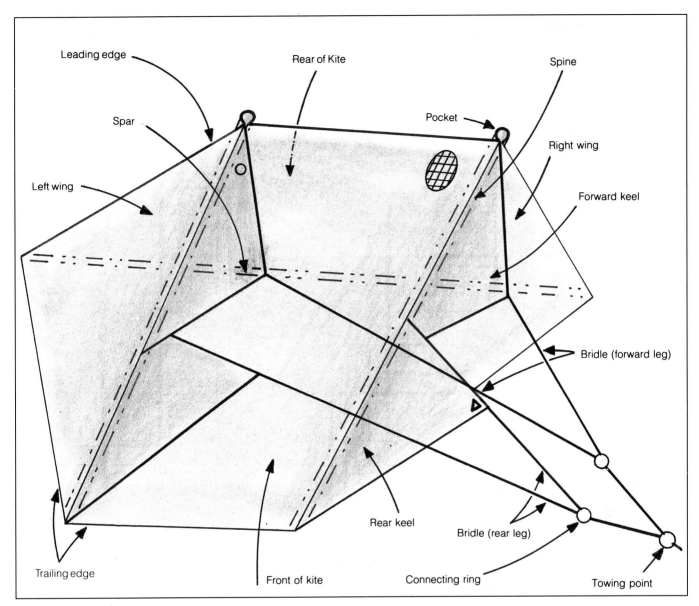

Leading edge · Rear of Kite · Spine · Spar · Pocket · Right wing · Left wing · Forward keel · Bridle (forward leg) · Bridle (rear leg) · Rear keel · Connecting ring · Towing point · Front of kite · Trailing edge

The most commonly used words in the vocabulary of kite making are shown in the illustration above; this should help you become familiar with the terminology. Wherever possible, use the materials as listed. And do read the manufacturer's instructions right through before making a kite, but beware that the illustrations are not always true to scale.

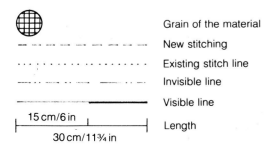

Grain of the material
New stitching
Existing stitch line
Invisible line
Visible line
15 cm/6 in — 30 cm/11¾ in Length

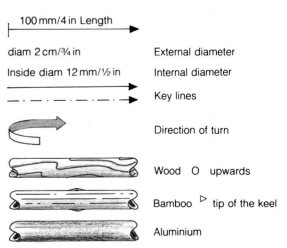

100 mm/4 in Length
diam 2 cm/¾ in — External diameter
Inside diam 12 mm/½ in — Internal diameter
Key lines
Direction of turn
Wood   O upwards
Bamboo ▷ tip of the keel
Aluminium

Eddy

The Eddy is a very effective kite, easy to make in the tyvek version. William A. Eddy invented this bow-type kite in 1891, and what made his invention sensational was that the kite was stable in flight even without a tail. It is prevented from breaking away in one direction by the loosely fitting sail and the dihedral form.

As a child I concentrated on this type of kite, also known as a Malay. Its good sail area to weight ratio makes the Eddy an excellent weight carrier, and its large, unbroken surface is ideal for decorating. Add a bow tail if flying the kite in gusty winds.

Materials:
2 pieces of dowelling, 150 cm/60 in long, diam 1 cm/⅖ in
150 cm/60 in tyvek, 150 cm/60 in wide or pergamyn
Nylon string, diam 0.1 cm/1/20 in
O-sealing ring, diam 3 cm/1¼ in
1 line tensioner
2 rings, diam 1 cm/⅖ in
Synthetic adhesive
1 swivel with carabiner

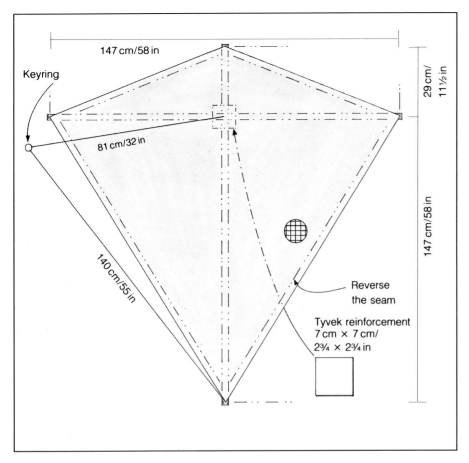

147 cm/58 in

Keyring

81 cm/32 in

29 cm/
11½ in

147 cm/58 in

140 cm/55 in

Reverse
the seam

Tyvek reinforcement
7 cm × 7 cm/
2¾ × 2¾ in

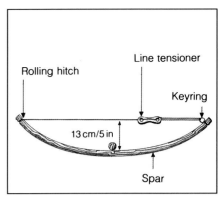

Rolling hitch

Line tensioner

Keyring

13 cm/5 in

Spar

Instructions:

First cut the dowelling to the desired length. Mark the middle of the spar with a pencil. An O-ring provides the best way of joining the two pieces because it allows you to dismantle the frame later. Other ways of connecting the pieces are shown in the fold-out section at the end of the book. Make a nick about 1 mm deep at the end of each spar with a file. The frame is spanned

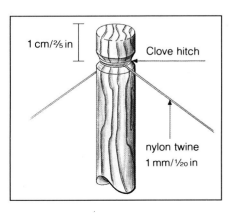

1 cm/⅖ in

Clove hitch

nylon twine
1 mm/1⁄20 in

with the nylon string (diam 0.1 cm/ 1⁄20 in) which is fixed to the notches using two half hitches or a clove hitch (see the fold-out at the end of the book). Make sure when spanning the kite that the frame does not bend because an asymmetrical Eddy will lead to unstable flight behaviour.

Next, lay out the tyvek on an even surface and place the frame spar on top. The spanned frame will serve as a stencil. Weigh it down and cut out the sail allowing a 2 cm/¾ in hem. Cut out a wedge shape from the tyvek over the ends of the dowelling. Fold over the hem and stick down with adhesive. Reinforce with a 7 × 7 cm/2¾ × 2¾ in piece of tyvek. Stick it on to the back of the sail at the height of the cross-joint.

Use scissors to cut a small hole in the sail at the cross-joint. The front bridle is now fixed to the frame with a reef knot. When tying up the rear bridle add a 1 cm/⅖ in ring. A tail can be attached to this ring later.

Another ring can be attached to the appropriate section of the bridle with a loop.

The dihedral of the Eddy is achieved by using a line to brace the spar. Fix a 1 cm/⅖ in ring to one end of the spar. The line is fixed to the other end. Thread it through a line tensioner to the ring and secure it to the tensioner. The curve on the spars can be altered by adjusting the tensioner.

Now you can begin to decorate the kite. Acrylic paints are best on tyvek. If you wish to add a bow-tail use a swivel with a carabiner hook. The swivel prevents the tail from becoming entwined.

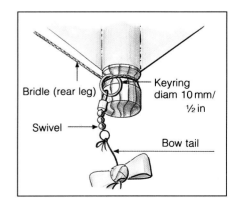

Bridle (rear leg)

Swivel

Keyring
diam 10 mm/
½ in

Bow tail

Eddy Train

In recent years, flying kite trains has become very popular. The kites are strung out like pearls on a string, creating a thrilling spectacle in the sky. The current world record for the number of kites flown from a single line was set in 1983 by a Japanese man who made it into *The Guinness Book of Records* by flying 5,581 kites.

The following instructions do not involve any sewing or gluing. The construction is extremely simple, enabling the whole family to join in. It is up to you to decide how many Eddys to tie to the line.

Materials per kite:
45 × 45 cm/17¾ × 17¾ in piece of tyvek or ripstop nylon
1 piece of dowelling, 100 cm/39½ in long, diam 4 mm/⅛ in
1 piece of aluminium tubing, 3 cm/ 1¼ in long, inner diam 4 mm/⅛ in
1 synthetic tube, inner diam 4 mm/ ⅛ in
Nylon string, diam 0.1 cm/¹⁄₂₀ in
Elastic band or O-ring

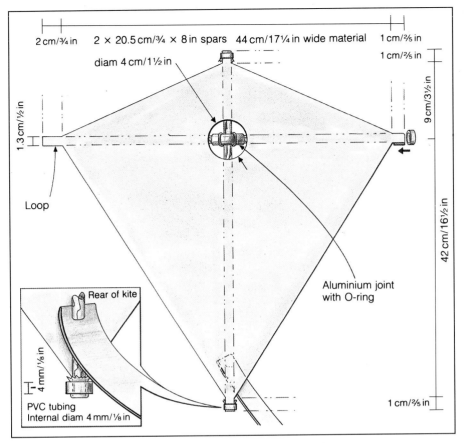

2 cm/¾ in   2 × 20.5 cm/¾ × 8 in spars   44 cm/17¼ in wide material   1 cm/⅖ in

diam 4 cm/1½ in

1 cm/⅖ in

9 cm/3½ in

1.3 cm/½ in

Loop

42 cm/16½ in

Aluminium joint
with O-ring

1 cm/⅖ in

Rear of kite

4 mm/⅛ in

PVC tubing
Internal diam 4 mm/⅛ in

Cut four rings from a piece of synthetic tubing. Once the loops have been placed round the nds of the dowelling the rings are pulled over them and fixed in place. This method allows you to produce many kites in a short time.

Three strip-tails, 4 cm/1½ in wide and 150 cm/59 in long, will keep the Eddys stable. A hole is punched into each of the strips. Before the sail is attached to the rear of the kite press the spine through the hole.

The individual kites are secured as follows: tie one bow for each kite in a 1 mm/¹⁄₂₀ in thick nylon wire at 130 cm/51 in intervals. Next, pass the line through the hole in each of the kites. Remove the upper part of the sail from the spine, and one of the spars from the aluminium bracket.

A loop drawn through the bow is passed over the spine and one half of the bracket. Once all the kites have been fixed to the line in this way, at 130 cm/51 in intervals, the rear bridle is secured to the foot of the kite with a clove hitch. The other end is knotted on the main string at an appropriate distance to the kite.

The uppermost kite flies at a distance of some 10 m/11 yd from the last. This adds to the stability of the kite train. The leading kite is equipped with a 3 m/3¼ yd long strip-tail. If the wind conditions are not steady you should use a leading kite that has greater pulling power, such as a 1 m/3¼ ft Eddy or a suitably sized box kite.

Instructions:

Begin by making the kite frame. A 42 cm/16½ in spine and two 20.5 cm/ 8 in spars form the basis. The jointing element for both spars is a 3 cm/ 1¼ in long aluminium tube with an inner diameter of 0.4 cm/⅛ in. Lay the aluminium tube on a firm base. A few blows with the peen of a hammer to the centre of the tubing will produce a 15° angle. The aluminium bracket is fixed to the spine with an elastic band or O-ring.

Since many sails are going to be cut out, it is advisable to use a stencil. Transfer the measurements of the sketch on to a piece of cardboard. The bridle will later be threaded through a 4 cm/1½ in large opening. Use a soldering iron to cut out the sail.

Fixing the sail to the frame is easy.

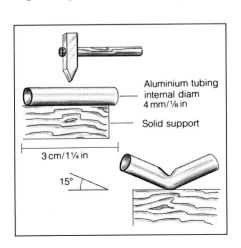

Aluminium tubing
internal diam
4 mm/⅛ in

Solid support

3 cm/1¼ in

15°

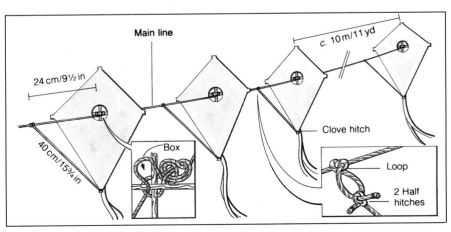

Main line

c. 10 m/11 yd

24 cm/9½ in

40 cm/15¾ in

Box

Clove hitch

Loop

2 Half
hitches

Hexagonal Kite

The hexagonal kite is one of the flat kites, and needs the stabilising effect of a kite tail. The Englishman W.R. Birt experimented with hexagonal kites as early as 1847, which he used to take meteorological readings at great altitudes. Making this kite does not present any difficulties. Tyvek or ripstop nylon can be used to cover it.

Materials:
4 × 1 m/4¼ × 1 yd ripstop nylon

6 pieces of dowelling, 1 m/3¼ ft long, diam 1 cm/²⁄₅ in
1 rigid synthetic disc, 1.5 cm/½ in thick, diam 6 cm/2⅓ in
1 ring, diam 2 cm/¾ in
Nylon string, diam 0.2 cm/¹⁄₁₀ in
6 m/6½ yd dacron, 1.5 cm/½ in wide, or seaming tape
1 piece of dacron, diam 5 cm/2 in

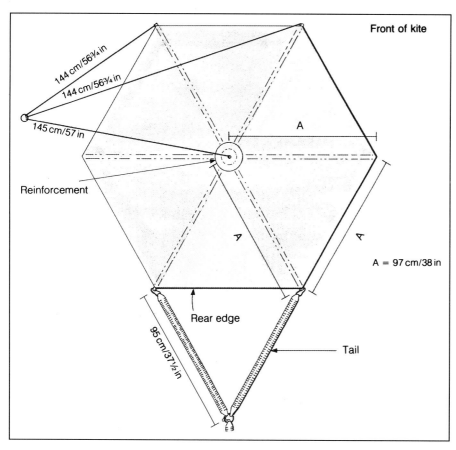

Front of kite

144 cm/56¾ in
144 cm/56¾ in
145 cm/57 in

Reinforcement

A

A = 97 cm/38 in

Rear edge

95 cm/37½ in

Tail

Instructions:

The sail of an hexagonal kite consists of two widths of nylon joined together. The widths, joined together with a lap seam, form a square with sides of about 2 m/2¼ yd each. Lay the nylon on an even surface. Transfer the outline of the hexagon on to the material. Allow an additional 2 cm/¾ in for the hem. To make the hem particularly strong reinforce it with dacron, which I prefer, or seaming tape. Dacron tape is available in 3 cm/1¼ in widths. Use scissors to trim it to the required width (see page 77).

For the spar pockets at the corners of the sail, 5 cm/2 in wide webbing is used. Webbing is a resistant material and prevents the spars from piercing the material.

The fitting of the pockets is explained in sewing techniques 9 and 10. A loop of ripstop nylon is pushed and sewn into both pockets of the front and rear edges of the kite. The bridle is attached to the two forward loops, and the tail is tied to the rear loops.

Use a soldering iron to cut out a circular piece of dacron, 5 cm/2 in wide, to be used for reinforcing. Sew the dacron on to the centre of the sail. A hole for the rear bridle, 1 cm/ ⅖ in wide, is cut into the middle of the sail with a soldering iron. If you want to be extra careful you can also add an eyelet (see sewing techniques 6, page 77).

The best way of connecting the spars is by using a rigid synthetic element. If you want to make things easier then join the three spars with a crossed lashing at the centre. The disadvantage of this method is that the kite cannot be dismantled.

When making my own rigid synthetic jointing elements I use nylon block which can be bought in various forms in specialist stores or kite shops. You can also use polyamide plates.

A 1.5 cm/½ in thick disc is sawn off from a round, rigid synthetic blank, diam 6 cm/2⅓ in. Accurately draw where the holes are to be drilled for the spars. The plastic must be positioned securely in a vice in order to ensure a smooth drilling action.

Next saw down the dowelling to the required length and trim the ends of the spars with a sharpener. Now you are ready to assemble the hexagonal kite. Make sure that the sail is tightly stretched on the frame. (Note: saw the spars a little longer than necessary, when fitting them later they can be trimmed symmetrically.) Attach the three-stringed bridle. The two upper strings are

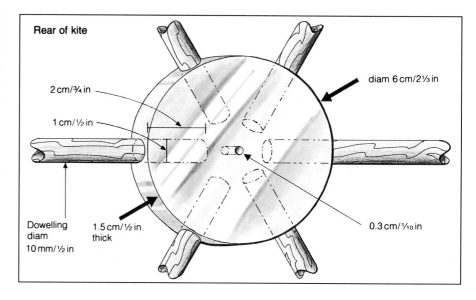

Rear of kite

2 cm/¾ in

1 cm/½ in

diam 6 cm/2⅓ in

Dowelling diam 10 mm/½ in

1.5 cm/½ in thick

0.3 cm/¹⁄₁₀ in

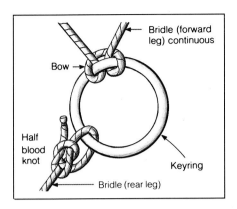

made of one continuous line. It is attached to its loops using a half blood knot. Make a loop halfway down its length. Then pass the rear bridle through the 3 mm/1/10 in drill hole and secure with a figure of eight knot. A ring is used to join up the three stringed bridle. Finally, the 12 m/13 yd long frayed tail should be secured to the kite with a half blood knot.

The hexagonal kite is now ready to fly. It can be made any size by adjusting the measurements to scale. To fly the kite in higher wind speeds the frame can be made of bamboo, fibre glass or carbon fibre.

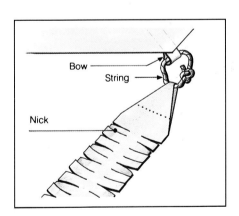

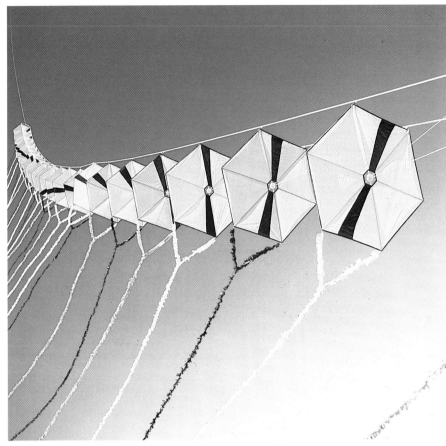

Hexagonal Train

The hexagonal kite can be flown in train formation by means of a clever bridling technique (the kite artist, Peter Malinski, has joined 50 kites together in this way). The detailed construction and styling ensure you get a fabulous effect, with the tails sounding like leaves rustling in a storm as you stand beneath the kites flying above you.

Launching this kite presents no problem. The individual kites are laid out on the ground, the tails arranged and then a leading line is fixed to the last kite. When the leading kite goes up it gradually draws the other kites after it, one after the other. Since the train develops enormous drag you will need several people to hold it in a fresh wind.

When constructing a kite train you should be clear about the likely drag. A hexagonal kite with 50 cm/19¾ in edges has a surface area of 0.75m²/ 8 ft². A train of 13 kites has a total sail area of some 10m²/12 yd². In a strong wind this train can develop a drag of over 30 kg/66 lb.

The measurements for the bridles given here are for a hexagonal kite with sides of 50 cm/19¾ in. The two upper bridles are continuous connecting lines that run from the first to the last kite. Pass these lines through the upper loops on your hexagonal kites. Do not knot the lines to the loops but secure them with thin fishing line. If there is a lot of drag this will prevent the lines from tearing. The interval between each kite should be equivalent to three times the length of each side of

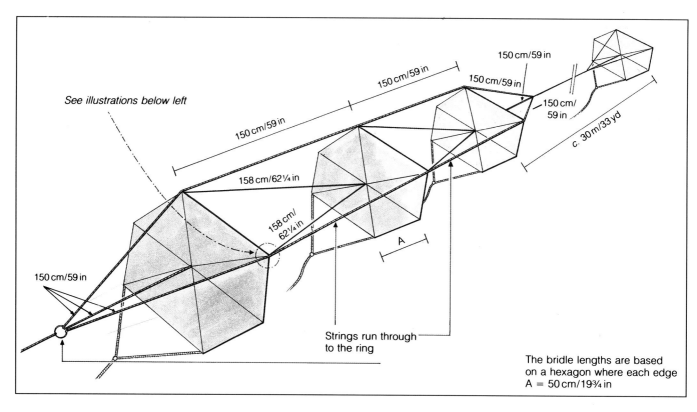

See illustrations below left

150 cm/59 in

150 cm/59 in

150 cm/59 in

150 cm/59 in

150 cm/59 in

c. 30 m/33 yd

158 cm/62¼ in

158 cm/62¼ in

150 cm/59 in

A

Strings run through
to the ring

The bridle lengths are based
on a hexagon where each edge
A = 50 cm/19¾ in

the hexagon (150 cm/59 in). The rear bridle is not continuous.

The first kite has a normal three-stringed bridle, as described on pages 28–9. The other kites in the train are equipped with a double lower bridle (see illustration). The length of the two rear bridles is 158 cm/62¼ in and is attached to the synthetic part with a short ribbon. The lower bridles are attached to the upper loops of the previous kite (see illustration). This form of bridling has one great advantage – the drag

of the rear bridle is not transferred to the synthetic fabric element of the previous kite.

Handling the hexagonal kite train is therefore much easier and the risk of the frame breaking is reduced. A three-stringed bridle is attached to the back of the final kite, to which the leading kite is secured. The leading kite should fly about 30 m/ 32¾ yd above the final kite in the train.

The distance between the kites will have to be adjusted for hexag-

onals with sides other than the 50 cm/19¾ in we have chosen. The length of the lower bridle L is then calculated as follows:

$$L = \sqrt{a^2 \times b^2}$$

where a = the length of the side of the hexagon; b = the distance between each kite (three times the length of the side).

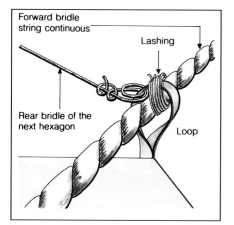

Forward bridle
string continuous

Lashing

Rear bridle of the
next hexagon

Loop

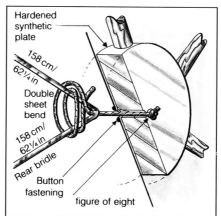

Hardened
synthetic
plate

158 cm/
62¼ in

Double
sheet
bend

158 cm/
62¼ in

Rear bridle

Button
fastening

figure of eight

Delta

A gentle breeze is all a delta kite needs for a good take-off. The beach is an ideal launching site, with its constant winds and wide open spaces. A powerful thermal will often be enough to have a delta soaring up to a great height, and its good flight performance has made it increasingly popular amongst kite fliers. Some kite makers even specialise in deltas, adjusting the wings and keel to produce even better flyers. The delta's predecessor was the flexible kite, invented in 1948 by Francis Rogallo.

Note: Should you still be experiencing difficulties in sewing ripstop nylon, the delta described below can be made from tyvek.

Materials:
150 × 100 cm/59 × 39¼ in ripstop nylon or tyvek
3 pieces of dowelling, diam 0.6 cm/ ¼ in
1 piece of dowelling, diam 0.7– 0.8 cm/¼–⅓ in
Eyelets, diam 0.5 cm/⅕ in
10 cm/4 in webbing 1 cm/⅖ in wide
2 D-rings, diam 1.4 cm/½ in

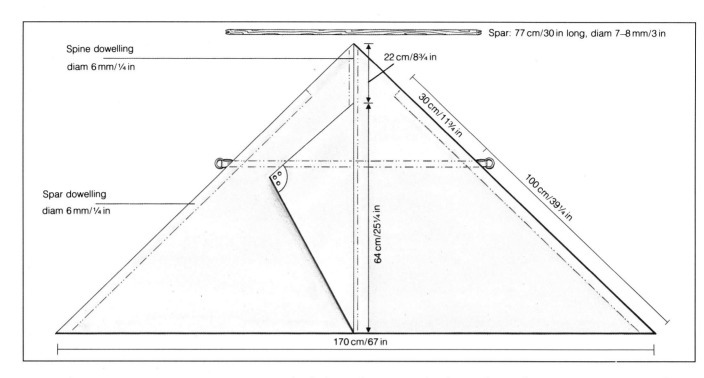

Spar: 77 cm/30 in long, diam 7–8 mm/3 in

Spine dowelling
diam 6 mm/¼ in

22 cm/8¾ in

30 cm/11¾ in

100 cm/39¼ in

Spar dowelling
diam 6 mm/¼ in

64 cm/25¼ in

170 cm/67 in

Instructions:

To keep cutting to a minimum the delta sail is made from one square of material. Draw the outline (91 × 91 cm/35¾ × 35¾ in) on to the rip-stop nylon. You should mark on all the additional measurements for the hems and pockets. The nylon is cut diagonally using a soldering iron. The outline of the keel should also be drawn on a piece of nylon, remembering the extra for the hem. The trailing and leading edges of the

wings both have hems, as do the outside edges of the keel.

To sew the pocket for the spine, the two wings are laid one on top of the other with their previously sewn hems facing inwards. The three parts, including the keel, are sewn up (see sewing techniques 11 and 12, page 77). The distance between the two seams will depend on the strength of the spine. For a 0.6 cm/¼ in thick spine, it should be 1.5 cm/½ in. If you have difficulties sewing

the pockets you can use pins to keep the material in place.

The delta is a semi-flexible kite. The cross-spar connects the outer spars, and is not rigidly fixed to the spine, so allowing the wings to adapt freely to the wind. This means you will be able to observe a variety of wing positions according to changes in the wind.

The pocket for the spar can be made in various ways. All kite makers have their own special method (compare sewing techniques). I prefer using a D-ring because it is very resistant and allows you to assemble the kite quickly. Mark the position of the rings on the leading edges. Each one is sewn on to the rear of the wings, along with a 1 cm/²⁄₅ in wide loop of webbing. If you use a sewing machine to sew on the webbing you may break the needle (it is sometimes necessary to use a stronger needle for thicker webbing). Instead of webbing you can use several layers of ribstop nylon.

The pockets for the edge-spars can be made from leftover ripstop nylon. You will need to cut out two rectangles (101 × 3 cm/39¾ × 1¼ in) and hem the sides. The rectangles

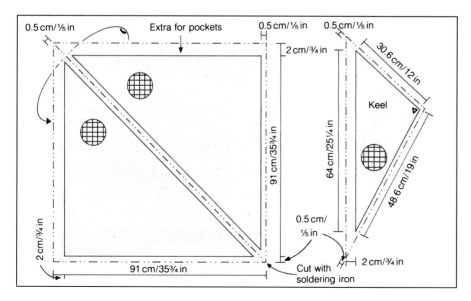

0.5 cm/⅕ in

Extra for pockets

0.5 cm/⅕ in

0.5 cm/⅕ in

2 cm/¾ in

30.6 cm/12 in

Keel

91 cm/35¾ in

64 cm/25¼ in

48.6 cm/19 in

2 cm/¾ in

0.5 cm/⅕ in

91 cm/35¾ in

Cut with soldering iron

2 cm/¾ in

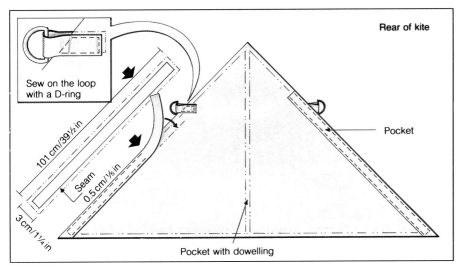

Rear of kite

Sew on the loop with a D-ring

101 cm/39½ in

Seam 0.5 cm/⅕ in

3 cm/1¼ in

Pocket with dowelling

Pocket

are then sewn on to the upper side of the wings. They should be sewn flush with the edges of the wings. Do not sew up the upper pockets of the edge-spars because if the dowelling breaks it can then be easily replaced. Push the spine into the appropriate pocket. Both ends of the pocket should then be sewn up.

You should not forget to reinforce the section of the keel where the eyelets have an extra layer of ripstop nylon or dacron. This will prevent the eyelets from being torn out of the sail, even in high winds.

The holes for the eyelets should be made with punching tongs. However, you can also use a soldering iron which has the advantage of automatically heat sealing the edges, and which gives the eyelet a firmer hold. In strong winds the line of the kite should be secured in the

upper eyelet, in average winds in the centre, and in light winds in the lower eyelet. Once the sewing work is complete and the eyelets are in place the edge-spars can be put into the pockets.

The 0.8 cm/⅓ in spar should be cut to length (77 cm/30⅓ in). Nick the ends with a saw or small file. To make these notches particularly strong you can dip the tips of the spars into wood adhesive. When dry, the adhesive prevents the spar from splintering, even under great pressure.

The delta is an excellent kite to fly in light winds. A hand launch is no problem at all, though the kite might behave erratically if there is turbulence just above ground level. To make the delta gain altitude let the line out quickly.

The spar is particularly pressured

in strong winds. For this reason you should have spares in different thicknesses to hand. I always have a bamboo spar ready for such occasions. Make sure that the bamboo is not too asymmetrical because the delta will not respond well to an uneven spread of weight.

If you want to alter the size of the delta you will have to adjust the measurements given here to scale. Obviously, this will also mean altering the thickness of the dowelling. For a delta with a span of over 3 m/ 3¼ yd, the edge-spars should be made of bamboo. For my largest delta, with a span of 10m/11 yd, I needed bamboo with a 3 cm/1¼ in diameter.

The largest delta I know of has a 45m²/53¾ yd² sail – its constructor uses two surf masts joined together for the spars. However, beware of constructing too large a delta because it will lose its elegance resulting in what are known as 'pinned back ears'.

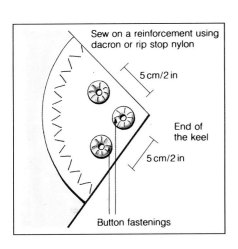

Sew on a reinforcement using dacron or rip stop nylon

5 cm/2 in

End of the keel

5 cm/2 in

Button fastenings

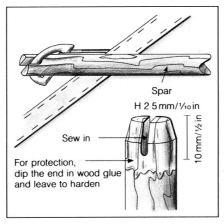

Spar
H 2 5 mm/⅒ in

Sew in

10 mm/½ in

For protection, dip the end in wood glue and leave to harden

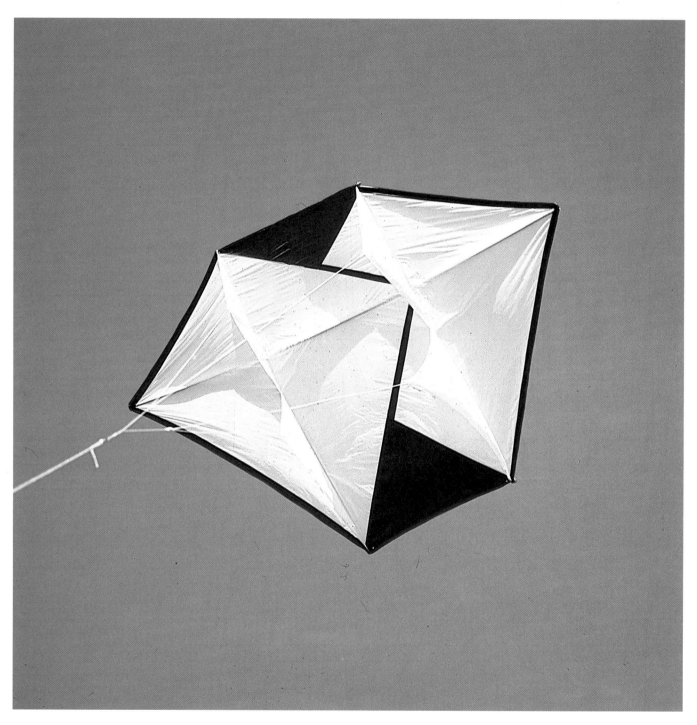

Flare

The flare is a recent development, whose crossbeam bends in flight so lending the kite stability. In addition, the keels on the underside make it stable at the sides. A wind-sock can be used as a drogue to give added stability. Note that the steep angle of the bridles develops enormous drag on the kite. This is excellent in light wind, though in gusty conditions it can be temperamental. In the right conditions it will fly above you, and at high altitudes will tend to glide.

Materials:
2 × 1 m/2¼ × 1 yd ripstop nylon
2 pieces of dowelling, 100 cm/
    39¼ in long, diam 0.6 cm/¼ in
1 piece of dowelling, 144 cm/56¾ in
    long, diam 0.7–0.8 cm/¼–⅓ in
10 cm/4 in webbing, 2 cm/¾ in wide
3 rings, diam 1.2 cm/¾ in

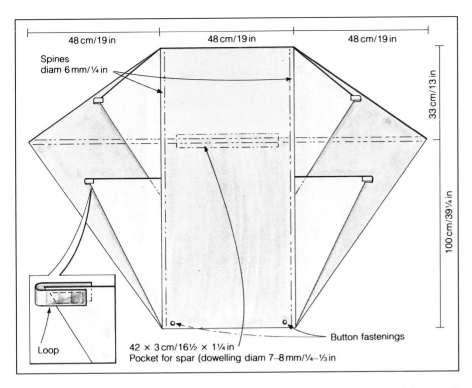

Spines
diam 6 mm/¼ in

48 cm/19 in 48 cm/19 in 48 cm/19 in

33 cm/13 in

100 cm/39¼ in

Loop

42 × 3 cm/16½ × 1¼ in
Pocket for spar (dowelling diam 7–8 mm/¼–⅓ in)

Button fastenings

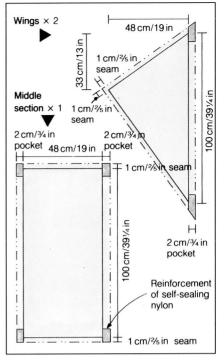

Wings × 2

48 cm/19 in

33 cm/13 in

1 cm/⅖ in
seam

Middle
section × 1

1 cm/⅖ in
seam

100 cm/39¼ in

2 cm/¾ in
pocket 48 cm/19 in 2 cm/¾ in
pocket

1 cm/⅖ in seam

100 cm/39¼ in

2 cm/¾ in
pocket

Reinforcement
of self-sealing
nylon

1 cm/⅖ in seam

Instructions:

The sail of a flare consists of two wings and a middle section. Draw the outlines of the sections on to the ripstop nylon and do not forget to add on extra for the hems and pockets. Cut out the sails with a soldering iron. Cut out two forward and two rear keels from the ripstop nylon.

Sew on the wings, middle section and keels to the appropriate edges (see sewing techniques 2, page 77).

Sew the pockets for the wing tips out of webbing (see sewing techniques 9). Cut out a 42 × 3 cm/16½ × 1¼ in section from a piece of

leftover ripstop nylon and hem all the edges. Sew the pocket on to the rear of the middle section.

Sew the two pockets for the spines (see sewing techniques 11 and 12, page 77). Put the wings and middle section together so that the forward sides show outwards and sew the two keels together. Tip: if you have problems sewing the pockets, pin the parts together first. The seams can also be glued together. Add loops to the tips of the keels, using several layers of nylon or narrow webbing.

Push the 1 m/1 yd long spines into the pockets and sew them up. The

cross-spar should be fitted tightly between the wing tips. The four-stringed connecting bridle is secured to the keels using a half blood knot. A ring will allow you to adjust the angle of flight. The rear bridle should be shortened in strong winds.

You will not need anyone to help you launch a flare, nor is there any problem in launching it by hand. However, you should always have a stronger cross-spar handy in case of high wind speeds. The windsock is hung from two small eyelets on the rear edge of the flare.

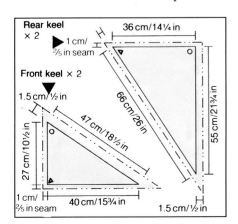

Rear keel
× 2

36 cm/14¼ in

1 cm/
⅖ in seam

Front keel × 2

1.5 cm/½ in

66 cm/26 in

47 cm/18½ in

55 cm/21¾ in

27 cm/10½ in

1 cm/
⅖ in seam

40 cm/15¾ in

1.5 cm/½ in

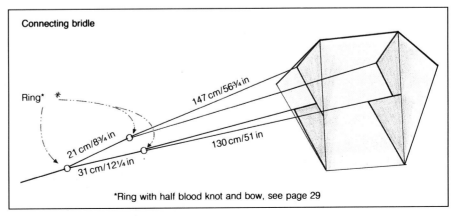

Connecting bridle

Ring*

147 cm/56¾ in

21 cm/8¾ in

31 cm/12¼ in

130 cm/51 in

*Ring with half blood knot and bow, see page 29

Flaero Train

I have called this train of 39 individual flares the double-Eddy flaero train on account of its overlapping Eddy motif. The train will even fly without a lead kite, resembling a ladder into the sky, almost vertical over its pilot's head.

Four bridle lines connect the individual flares. The keels are rein-forced with webbing before sewing up the sail. The two ends of the webbing form a loop. Sew this carefully together with the keels (see 13 and 14, page 77). Once all the kites in the train have been rein-forced in this way they are connected with four bridle lines.

Note: the forward bridles are 170 cm/ 67 in, the rear bridles 156 cm/61 in.

Now secure the connecting lines with half blood knots. The strain on the first kite depends on the length of the train. In my train the first 10 kites have 0.6 cm/¼ in thick connec-ting lines. As you move back to the final kite the thickness is gradually reduced to 0.1 cm/¹⁄₂₀ in. Also, the first six kites are fitted with a 0.6 cm/ ¼ in thick fibre glass rod. If you are using a lead kite to facilitate the launch, then the last flare should be fitted with a four-stringed bridle to secure the lead kite.

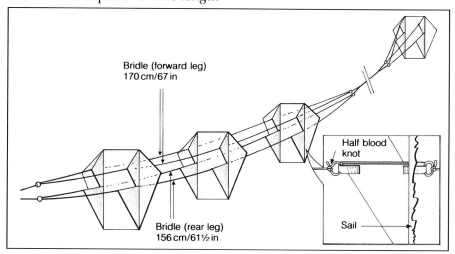

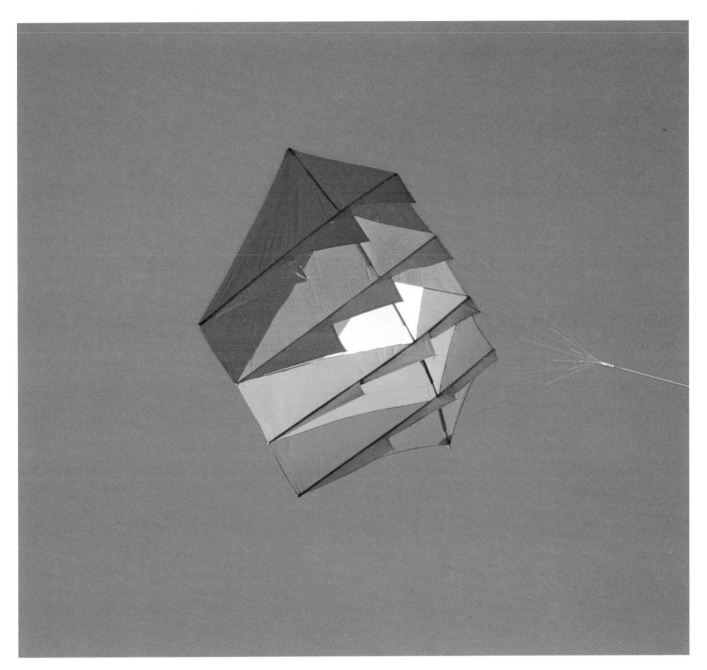

Multiflare

The multiflare is as excellent in light winds as is its little brother, but it can develop enormous drag even given moderate wind speeds (it is advisable to wear leather gloves when flying this kite to ensure the string does not cut into your hands). Its size can be varied and I once built a 32 m²/38¼ yd² multiflare which was quite capable of lifting two people off the ground.

The kite's geometric form allows for interesting graphic styling. Before starting on its construction draw its outline on a piece of paper and develop your own pattern. The trimming of the 12 bridles looks complicated, but the following instructions show how this can be achieved without difficulty. The multiflare should be flown with a windsock in gusty conditions.

Materials:
9 m²/10¾ yd² ripstop nylon
12 m/13 yd synthetic tubing, diam
  1.5 cm/½ in or
6 pieces of dowelling, 2 m (2 yd)
  long, diam 1–1.2 cm/½ in (2 pieces
  for the cross-spar)
Dacron for reinforcing
12 cm/4¾ in webbing, 2 cm/¾ in
  wide
12 eyelets, diam 0.5 cm/⅕ in
Self-adhesive nylon
1 ring, diam 2.5 cm/1 in

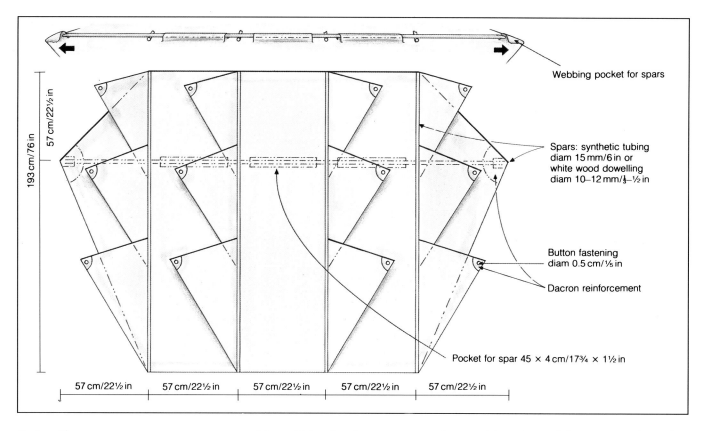

Webbing pocket for spars

Spars: synthetic tubing diam 15 mm/6 in or white wood dowelling diam 10–12 mm/⅜–½ in

Button fastening diam 0.5 cm/⅕ in

Dacron reinforcement

Pocket for spar 45 × 4 cm/17¾ × 1½ in

193 cm/76 in

57 cm/22½ in

57 cm/22½ in | 57 cm/22½ in | 57 cm/22½ in | 57 cm/22½ in | 57 cm/22½ in

Instructions:

PVC tubing or 1.2 cm/½ in dowelling are suitable for making the multiflare frame. The synthetic tubing is flexible, so giving the kite its stabilising dihedral form.

First, cut out the three middle sections and the wings. Take care to add on extra for the hems and pockets. Make the hems on the outer edges (see sewing technique 2, page 77). Sew pockets made of 2 cm/¾ in-

wide webbing for the spars on to the rear of the sails. Cut out three strips of ripstop nylon (45 × 4 cm/17¾ × ⅛ in) and hem the edges. Sew the pockets, as directed, on to the middle sections. Cut out four forward, four middle and four rear keels from the ripstop nylon (use a stencil), and sew in 5 mm/1⅕ in wide dacron reinforcing into the keel hems (see sewing technique 2). The tips of the keels should be reinforced

with a piece of dacron or nylon. The eyelets are then put into the tips of the keel to secure the bridles.

Use self-adhesive nylon (3 × 4 cm/1¼ × 1½ in) to reinforce the corners of the middle sections and wings. They can also be glued on. Stick on the reinforcing so that, later, it is on the inside of the pockets.

Anyone who is experienced in sewing up ripstop nylon can sew together the sails and keels (see

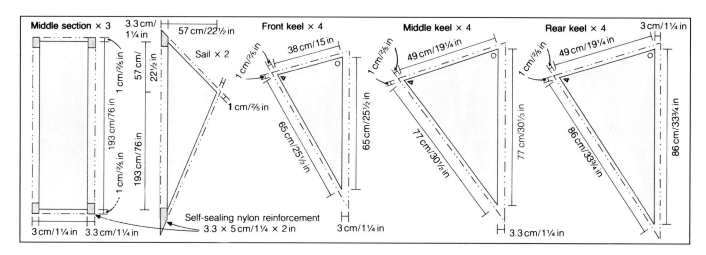

Middle section × 3

3.3 cm/1¼ in

57 cm/22½ in

Sail × 2

1 cm/⅖ in

1 cm/⅖ in

57 cm/22½ in

193 cm/76 in

1 cm/⅖ in

193 cm/76 in

1 cm/⅖ in

3 cm/1¼ in   3.3 cm/1¼ in

Self-sealing nylon reinforcement 3.3 × 5 cm/1¼ × 2 in

Front keel × 4

1 cm/⅖ in

38 cm/15 in

65 cm/25½ in

65 cm/25½ in

3 cm/1¼ in

Middle keel × 4

1 cm/⅖ in

49 cm/19¼ in

77 cm/30½ in

77 cm/30⅓ in

3.3 cm/1¼ in

Rear keel × 4

3 cm/1¼ in

1 cm/⅖ in

49 cm/19¼ in

86 cm/33¾ in

86 cm/33¾ in

sewing techniques 11 and 12, page 77). Less experienced kite makers should first glue the joints together before they start sewing. Before sewing the first seam, the sail sections should be positioned in such a way that the forward sides face outwards. The width of the pockets will depend on the thickness of the spars. For synthetic tubing 1.5 cm/½ in thick it will be about 3 cm/1½ in wide. Remember the extra for seam. For a 1.2 cm/½ in dowelling spine the pocket should be about 2 cm/¾ in wide.

Check that the forward edges of the middle and rear keels run inwards (see sketch). Once the pockets for the spines have been sewn stitch up the opening. Cut the PVC tubing to length and push into the pockets. Sew up the pockets. Should you wish to remove the spine later, or replace it with another, make a small opening in the pocket with a soldering iron.

Cut the PVC spars to length and plug the ends with dowelling. Shape the plug conically with a knife and glue into the PVC tubing. The spar should be fitted tightly between the pockets of the wing tips.

If you are using a two-part wooden spar then this need only be trimmed with a knife or file. It can be jointed with aluminium tubing, see jointing techniques 9 page 78.

Trimming the bridle is simple: lay the finished kite on the floor and weigh it down as illustrated. A ring

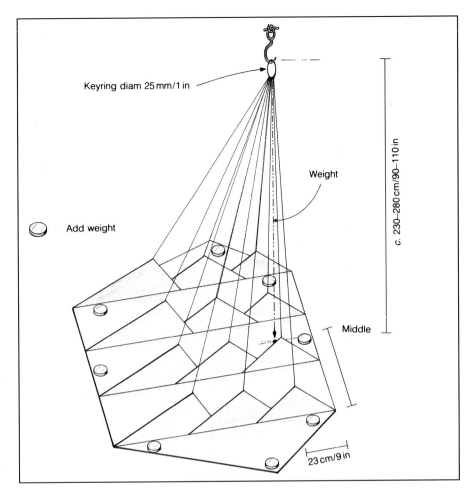

Keyring diam 25 mm/1 in

Add weight

Weight

c. 230–280 cm/90–110 in

Middle

23 cm/9 in

is secured 2.3 × 2.8 m/2½ × 3 yd above the kite (from the ceiling say). The position of the ring is determined by a plumb line that hangs over the point, as shown in the illustration.

The bridles are fixed to the keels with half blood knots. They are then pulled tightly upwards and attached to the ring. If you want to do things carefully then use a connecting bridle as this will allow you to trim the multiflare later when preparing to fly the kite.

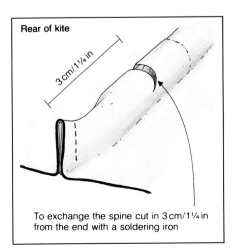

Rear of kite

3 cm/1¼ in

To exchange the spine cut in 3 cm/1¼ in from the end with a soldering iron

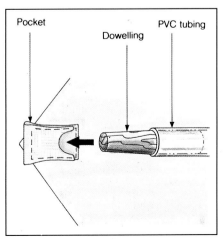

Pocket

Dowelling

PVC tubing

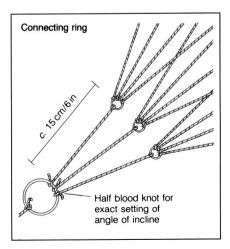

Connecting ring

c. 15 cm/6 in

Half blood knot for exact setting of angle of incline

Nagasaki Hata

The Nagasaki Hata (fighting kite) has a long tradition. Although Japan was closed to foreigners between 1639 and 1854, Dutch traders were allowed to use the port of Nagasaki. Early in the 17th century they stopped here on the way back from India and introduced the Japanese to the fighting kite. They gave it its traditional colours of red, white and blue, as found on the Dutch flag.

The Nagasaki Hata is very manoeuvrable, but when building it care must be taken to ensure that the correct symmetry and balance are achieved. Providing this is done the fighting kite can even be flown when the wind is still, as Japanese kite specialists have shown. The kite maintains its plane angle (stability) by using the wind pressure or the drag on the line. If the string is relaxed the kite will tumble, but the skilful fighting kite pilot overcomes this loss in height at a particular position when, with a pull on the line, he gets the kite back to its stable flight path. The direction of the trajectory is always the same as the direction shown by the tip of the Hata. It is even possible to fly the kite with the tip against the wind.

In order to release and gather in the string as quickly as possible it is not wound on a reel but laid out on the ground.

Flying fighting kites is a Japanese sport. Every year in springtime there are many fighting kite competitions held in and around Nagasaki. The kite string is coated in a paste made with powdered glass, which when given a sharp tug will cut through the opponent's string. A shout of

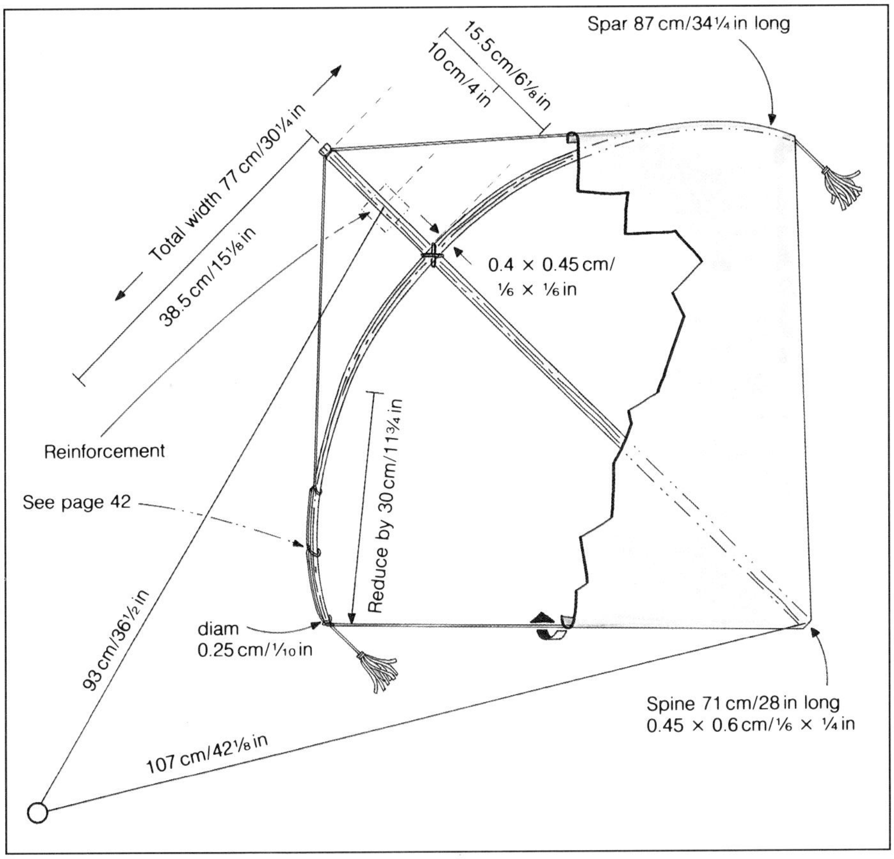

Spar 87 cm/34¼ in long
15.5 cm/6⅛ in
10 cm/4 in
Total width 77 cm/30¼ in
38.5 cm/15⅛ in
0.4 × 0.45 cm/
⅙ × ⅙ in
Reinforcement
See page 42
Reduce by 30 cm/11¾ in
diam
0.25 cm/⅒ in
93 cm/36½ in
Spine 71 cm/28 in long
0.45 × 0.6 cm/⅙ × ¼ in
107 cm/42⅛ in

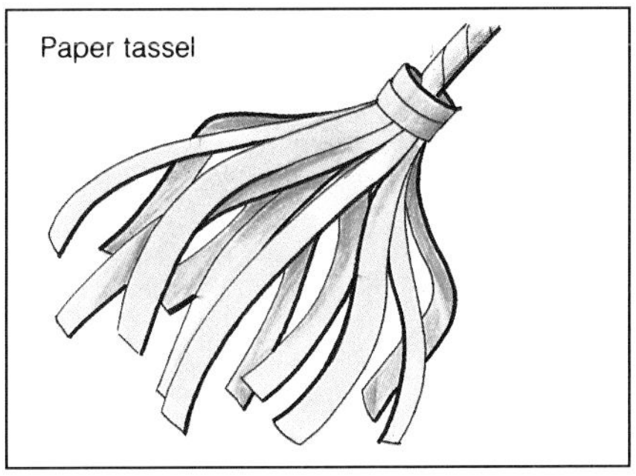

Paper tassel

'Katsuro' goes up as a severed Hata falls to the ground. Then a race begins with the first person reaching the grounded kite becoming its new owner.

Materials:

0.7 m²/7½ ft² kite paper (pergamyn)
Split bamboo, 71 cm/28 in long, 0.45 × 0.4 cm/⅙ × ⅙ in
Split bamboo, 87 cm/34¼ in long, 0.45 × 0.4 cm/⅙ × ⅙ in or fibre glass rod, diam 0.3 cm/⅒ in
Nylon string, diam 0.5 mm/¹⁄₅₀ in

Instructions:

Anyone who values traditions should make the Nagasaki Hata out of bamboo. The elements for the frame can be made by splitting a 2.5 cm/1 in thick bamboo cane (see splitting bamboo, page 17).

Use a knife, steadily trimming the 0.45 × 0.4 cm/⅙ × ⅙ in thick spar down to 0.25 × 0.25 cm/⅒ × ⅒ in at the ends. This process should begin about 30 cm/11¾ in from the end. Beware when choosing the spar as any unevenness in the bamboo can influence the symmetry of the curved cane. After they have been fashioned with the knife the bamboo rods should be sanded down to avoid splinters.

A 0.3 cm/⅒ in fibre glass rod can be used in place of the bamboo spar. There is then no need to trim the ends. It should, however, be remembered that fibre glass is heavier than bamboo and will need more wind.

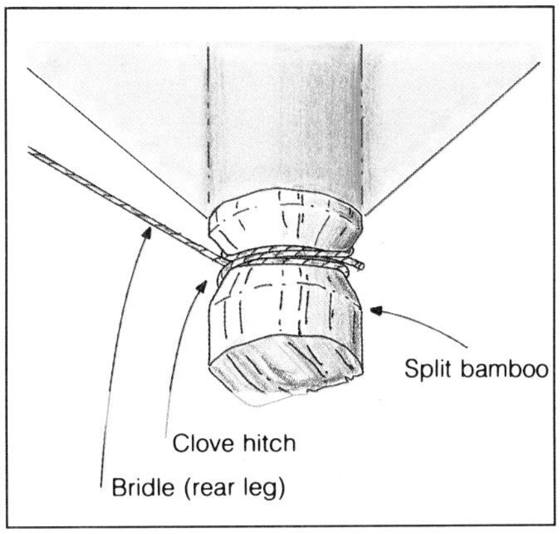

Split bamboo
Clove hitch
Bridle (rear leg)

Join the spars by cross lashing them in the appropriate position. Beware: it is absolutely essential at this point to check for balance and symmetry. The narrower side of the spar (0.4 cm/⅙ in) is laid on to the spine. The frame is spanned by a nylon thread (diam 0.5 mm/¹⁄₅₀ in). Begin at the base with a clove hitch. Secure the thread with clove hitches to the tips of the wings and then stretch them backwards. The tethering thread is also secured to the spar with two half hitches each.

The finished kite frame is laid on to the kite paper with the spar downwards. If you want a coloured covering then stick the appropriate parts together first. Use the span of the frame as a stencil and cut out the paper (allowing 1.5 cm/½ in for the seam). Lay the seam around the tethering thread and stick on. Glue on a 3 cm/1¼ in sized piece to reinforce the point where the bridle will be on the back of the sail. Attach the nylon bridle: the forward bridle is 93 cm/36½ in, the rear 107 cm/42⅛ in.

For additional stability a paper tassel is fixed to each of the Hata's wing tips. Make these from strips of paper *c.* 8 cm/3⅐ in wide rolled up and cut into strips with scissors. The tassel is held together with a staple.

If you have never flown a fighting kite before you should make sure you have someone to help with the launch. Lay out an extra 5–10 m/16½–32¾ ft of string on the ground. A high-start launch can help get round initial steering problems encountered with this single stringed dirigible kite.

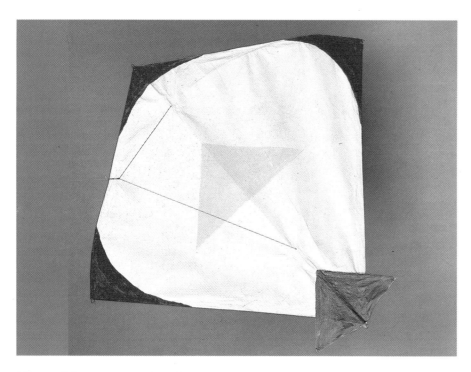

Indian Fighting Kite

The Indian fighting kite is not much different from its Japanese counterpart — instead of having tassels at the side it is stabilized by a tail fin. It certainly requires a little experience to fly this fast and sensitive kite. A more stable flight can be achieved on practice runs by fixing a small weight (plasticine, for example) to the tip of the kite which makes it react more slowly to the string being released or pulled in. Fixing the weight to the spine in the direction of the stabilizer will make the fighting kite less stable.

Materials:

0.6 m²/6½ yd² kite paper (pergamyn)
Split bamboo, 73 cm/28¾ in long, 0.3 × 0.3 cm/¹⁄₁₀ × ¹⁄₁₀ in, or
Fibre glass rod, diam 0.2 cm/¹⁄₁₀₀ in
Nylon thread, diam 0.5 mm/¹⁄₅₀ in

Instructions:

To make the Indian fighting kite you should follow the instructions for the Nagasaki Hata exactly. The spar is trimmed down towards the ends to 0.15 cm/¹⁄₁₅ in. Attach the spar to the spine narrow face down and secure with a cross lashing.

A fibre glass rod may be used in place of the bamboo spar. Glue the kite reinforcement to the rear of the kite. Secure the forward bridle to the crosspoint of the frame. The rear bridle is secured to the spine with a reef knot. Cut out the stabilizer. Glue a 0.1 cm/¹⁄₂₀ in thick piece of split bamboo to each of the upper edges on the stabilizer. Glue it to the front of the kite with the bamboo facing inwards.

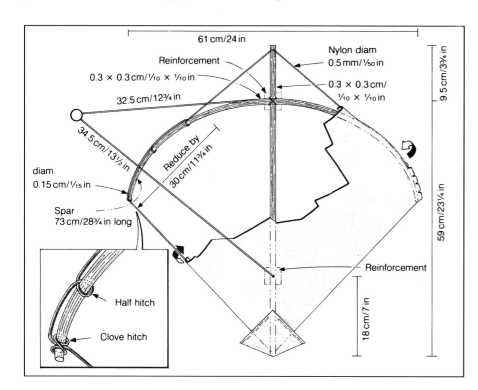

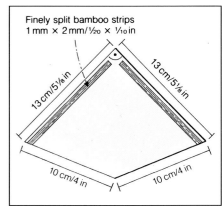

Sanjo Rokkaku

For over 250 years people in Shirone (Japan) have battled for fame and honour with the Sanjo Rokkaku. Fifty kite teams from two villages try to sever their opponents' strings. They take up positions on opposite banks of a 70 m/76½ yd wide canal, and having skilfully trimmed the bridle steer the fighting kite across to the opponents' bank. The trimming of the bridle remains a team secret.

The Sanjo Rokkaku must be made with enormous care and is built to a standard height of 330 cm/137¾ in. Precise adjustments to the bridle and the trimming of the bow-string can make the Rokkaku into the perfect fighting kite. To make it possible for it to be flown by a single person I have reduced its height to 210 cm/82¾ in. Also if the spine is removed and the kite rolled up it can be transported without difficulty. And finally, always wear gloves when flying the Rokkaku to avoid injury from cuts from the string.

Materials:
4.5 × 1 m/5 × 1¼ ft ripstop nylon
Leftover dacron
1 piece of dowelling, 210 cm/82¾ in long, diam 1.3 cm/½ in
2 pieces of dowelling, 176 cm/69¼ in long, diam 1 cm/²⁄₅ in

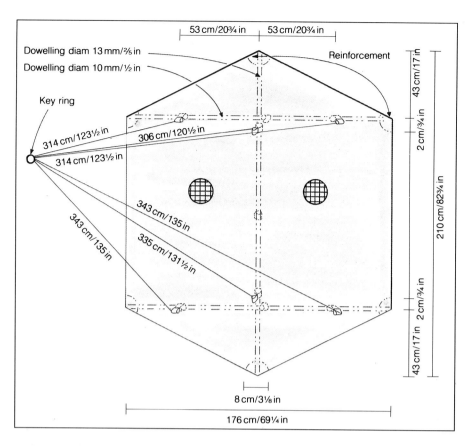

Dowelling diam 13 mm/⅖ in
Dowelling diam 10 mm/½ in

Key ring

Reinforcement

53 cm/20¾ in   53 cm/20¾ in

43 cm/17 in

2 cm/¾ in

210 cm/82¾ in

2 cm/¾ in

43 cm/17 in

314 cm/123½ in
306 cm/120½ in
314 cm/123½ in
343 cm/135 in
343 cm/135 in
335 cm/131½ in

8 cm/3⅛ in

176 cm/69¼ in

Materials continued:
1.5 m/1¾ yd webbing, 1.3 cm/½ in wide
1 ring, diam 2.5 cm/1 in
3 rings, diam 1.2 cm/½ in
22 m/24 yd nylon line, diam 3 mm/¹⁄₁₀ in
2 line tensioners

Instructions:
Cut two widths of ripstop nylon, each 220 cm/78¾ in long. Sew the cloths together at the longer side using a lap seam (see sewing techniques 1). On an even surface, draw the outline of the Rokkaku on to the nylon allowing 2 cm/¾ in for the hem. The lap seam should run vertically.

Use a soldering iron to cut out six pieces of dacron reinforcement (diam 8 cm/3⅛ in). Stitch these to the rear of the sail as illustrated.

Hem the six sides of the sail with a 1.5 cm/½ in wide strip of dacron (see sewing techniques 2, page 77).

Cut out pockets for the spars from 2.5 cm/1 in wide webbing and stitch to the rear of the sail (see sewing techniques 9, page 77). Remember when sewing the pockets that the spine has a diameter of 1.3 cm/½ in and the spar a diameter of 1 cm/⅖ in. Add loops to the side pockets (see sewing techniques 9 and 10, page 77). At the base of the kite a loop made of 1.3 cm/½ in wide webbing replaces a pocket (see sewing techniques 4, page 77). Secure a 1.2 cm/½ in ring to the loop. Next, sew on the six loops for the spars and securing the bridles. Proceed exactly as directed on the illustration: form two loops from a 13 cm/5⅛ in long piece of webbing and make a dart. Using a soldering iron, cut four holes, two vertical and two horizontal (1.4 cm/½ in each) into the sail (see illustration.)

Pass the loops through them from above and stitch to the sail.

Cut out round reinforcements diam 6 cm/2⅓ in. Cut 1.4 cm/½ in slits with a soldering iron and push the dacron over the loops. Join the dacron and sail with two zigzag seams. The advantage of this double looping is that the power of the bridles is transferred directly to the spars and the kite can still be dismantled.

If you do not have any 1.3 cm/½ in wide webbing then several layers of ripstop nylon will fulfil the same function. Strong, self-adhesive nylon can also be used in place of dacron. But use more stitching to provide greater hold. Sew a 3 cm/

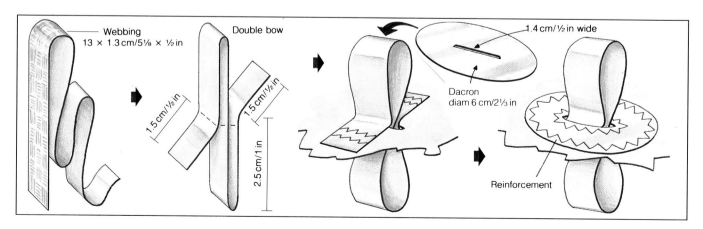

Webbing
13 × 1.3 cm/5⅛ × ½ in

Double bow

1.5 cm/½ in

1.5 cm/½ in

2.5 cm/1 in

1.4 cm/½ in wide

Dacron
diam 6 cm/2⅓ in

Reinforcement

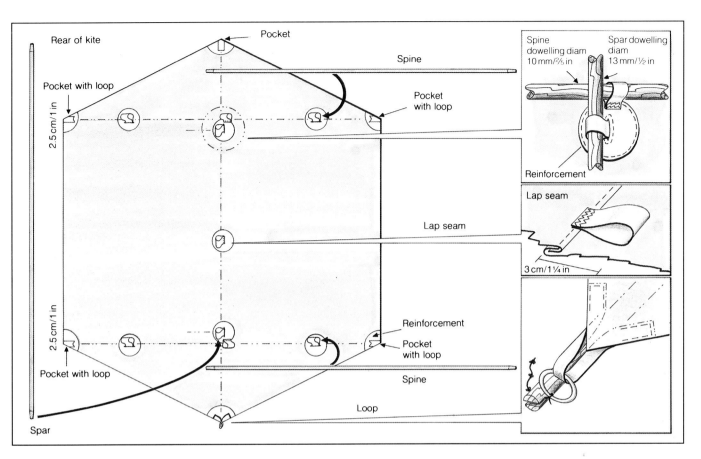

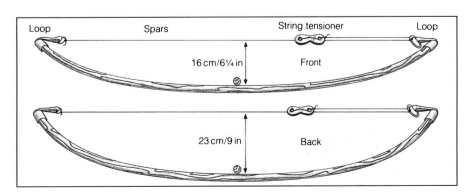

1¼ in loop on to the rear of the vertical lap seam. The loop should be in the middle of the sail and is used for housing the spine. Sew a further two loops on to the sail for the spars (see illustration for exact position). A line tensioner is also used on the spine. A 15 cm/6 in long 0.4 cm/⅙ in string is bound to the base of the kite.

Tie 8 knots into the string at 1.5 cm/½ in intervals. Cut the spine to the required length. Nick one end with a saw to a depth of 1.5 cm/½ in. The length of the spar should be calculated to allow several positions for the line tensioner. Saw both spars to length. They should sit tightly between the pockets.

The Rokkaku is not only an excellent kite in light winds, but displays good flying qualities in strong winds, too. For this reason I use a second rod made of carbon fibre so that I can fly the kite in various wind speeds. The spars of the Rokkaku are tensed with a bow string (see illustration).

Knot a 0.3 cm/1/10 in string to a side loop, then secure a 1.2 cm/½ in ring to the opposite loop. The string is passed through the line tensioner to the ring and back to the tensioner again. By adjusting the position of the line tensioner you can alter the curve of the kite.

Altering the bow strings alters the stability of the kite. The basic rule is the rear spar is more strongly curved than the forward spar. With a bow of 16 cm/6¾ in and 23 cm/9 in the Rokkaku will enjoy a stable flight.

Attach bridles made of 0.3 cm/1/10 in wide nylon string. The bridles are connected with a 2.5 cm/1 in ring. If the kite is meant to react more quickly in competition, reduce the curve on the rear spar.

The rules of competition are strictly laid down. Information is available from The Kite Society of Great Britain, 31 Grange Road, Ilford, Essex IG1 1EU. The American Kitefliers' Association can be contacted at 1559 Rockville Pike, Rockville, Maryland 20852.

45

Janggaan

Kite making and flying is a centuries old tradition in Bali, and is thought to have arrived here from China over 2,000 years ago. In Bali the Janggaan is built 10 m/11 yd tall, its bird-like head being decorated with hibiscus blossoms and colourful grasses. With its 80 m/87½ yd long and 5 m/5½ yd wide tail it looks like a gigantic snake in the sky, the long tail symbolising an eternal supply of food. The Janggaan is traditionally fitted with two 5 m/5½ yd whizzers, producing a loud but pleasant humming sound when one of these giants is hovering overhead. Balinese kites are made only in black, red, yellow, orange and white. To avoid launching problems the Janggaan should be given a high start.

Materials:

6 × 1 m/6½ × 1 yd tyvek
2 split bamboo rods, 136 cm/53½ in long, 0.8 × 0.5 cm/⅓ × ⅕ in, or
Fibre glass tubing, diam 0.3 cm/ 1/10 in
1 split bamboo rod, 140 cm/55⅛ in long, 0.9 × 0.5 cm/⅓ × ⅕ in, or
Fibre glass tubing, diam 0.6 cm/¼ in
2 split bamboo rods, 30 cm/11¾ in long, 0.2 cm × 0.15 cm/1/10 × 1/15 in
2 split bamboo rods, 37 cm/14½ in long, 0.2 × 0.2 cm/1/10 × 1/10 in
2 pieces of dowelling, 70 cm/27½ in long, diam 0.5 cm/⅕ in
2 pieces of dowelling, 66 cm/26 in, diam 0.4 cm/⅛ in
1 piece of dowelling, 67 cm/26½ in long, diam 0.3 cm/1/10 in
PVC tubing, 5 cm/2 in long, diam 0.5 cm/2 in
PVC tubing, 5 cm/2 in long, diam 0.4 cm/⅛ in

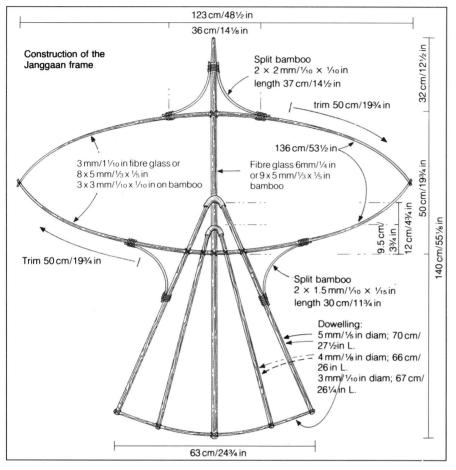

Construction of the Janggaan frame

123 cm/48½ in

36 cm/14⅛ in

Split bamboo
2 × 2 mm/¹⁄₁₀ × ¹⁄₁₀ in
length 37 cm/14½ in

trim 50 cm/19¾ in

32 cm/12½ in

3 mm/1¹⁄₁₀ in fibre glass or
8 × 5 mm/⅓ × ⅕ in
3 × 3 mm/¹⁄₁₀ × ¹⁄₁₀ in on bamboo

136 cm/53½ in

Fibre glass 6 mm/¼ in
or 9 × 5 mm/⅓ × ⅕ in
bamboo

50 cm/19¾ in

140 cm/55⅛ in

9.5 cm/3¾ in

12 cm/4¾ in

Trim 50 cm/19¾ in

Split bamboo
2 × 1.5 mm/¹⁄₁₀ × ¹⁄₁₅ in
length 30 cm/11¾ in

Dowelling:
5 mm/⅕ in diam; 70 cm/
27½ in L.
4 mm/⅛ in diam; 66 cm/
26 in L.
3 mm/¹⁄₁₀ in diam; 67 cm/
26¼ in L.

63 cm/24¾ in

Materials continued:
Polystyrene ball, *c.* diam 8 cm/3⅛ in
Nylon string, diam 0.1 cm/¹⁄₂₀ in
Fishing line; pergamyn for fringing
1 ring, diam 12 mm/½ in

Instructions:
The Balinese make the Janggaan's
frame from bamboo. As a rule, the
kite can not be dismantled which
makes transport a problem. The
Janggaan presented here is 140 cm/
55⅛ in long and 123 cm/48½ in wide
which makes it possible to transport
it by car. The elliptically bowed sail
and the spine can be made either of
split bamboo or fibre glass. I recom-
mend bamboo because, despite its
low weight, it displays good elas-
ticity and toughness.

The first step is to split a bamboo
rod to make two strips of 136 cm/
4½ ft each. Trim the 0.8 × 0.5 cm/⅓
× ⅕ in rods down to 0.3 × 0.3 cm/¹⁄₁₀
× ¹⁄₁₀ in at the ends. Make the spine
from split bamboo (140 cm/55⅛ in
long). Punch a hole into the two
5 cm/3 in pieces of tubing with punching tongs. Slide the tubing over the
spine. Secure the spar to the spine
with a cross lashing. Bind the ends
of the spar together.

Saw two 0.5 and 0.4 cm/⅛–⅕ in
pieces of dowelling to length (70–
66 cm/27½–26 in). Secure the dowelling with the tubing to the spine and
fix to rear spar with a cross lashing
(see illustration). Use a 0.3 cm/¹⁄₁₀ in
piece of dowelling to connect the
five tail rods. Make four sticks, two
each of 0.2 × 0.2 cm/¹⁄₁₀ × ¹⁄₁₀ in and
0.2 × 0.15 cm/¹⁄₁₀ × ¹⁄₁₅ in finely split
bamboo. See illustration for positioning of the split sticks for the head
and side. The sticks can be bent over
boiling water before working them.
You can use narrow rattan in place of
the bamboo sticks. Secure the bamboo parts to the frame with fishing
line.

The sail of the Janggaan is made of
tyvek (note that the spine is on the
fore of the sail in the elliptical
section). The elliptical part of the
frame is formed first. Use the ellipse
as a stencil to cut out the sail
(allowing 2.5 cm/1 in extra for the
hem). Where it meets the spars and
curves cut a slit of 2.5 cm/1 in in the

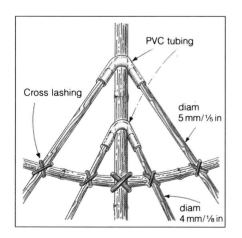

Cross lashing

PVC tubing

diam
5 mm/⅕ in

diam
4 mm/⅛ in

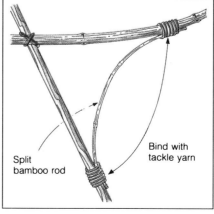

Split
bamboo rod

Bind with
tackle yarn

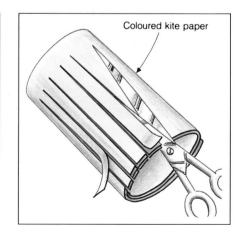

Coloured kite paper

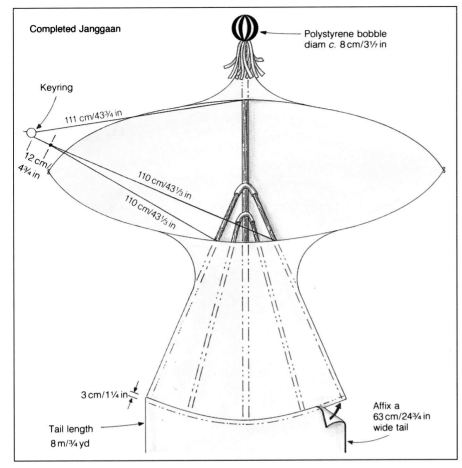

Completed Janggaan

Polystyrene bobble diam *c.* 8 cm/3½ in

Keyring

111 cm/43¾ in

12 cm/4¾ in

110 cm/43⅓ in

110 cm/43⅓ in

3 cm/1¼ in

Tail length 8 m/¾ yd

Affix a 63 cm/24¾ in wide tail

and sail can be decorated with acrylic paint. The 63 cm/24¾ in wide and 8 m/8¾ yd long tyvek tail is glued directly on to the foot of the kite (3cm/1⅛ in overlap). The tail is decorated in the same way as the sail.

The three connecting stringed bridle made of 0.1 cm/1/20 in nylon string is secured to the spine and bridle with a round turn and two half hitches. Using a ring at this point makes any future adjustment to the bridle considerably easier.

The Janggaan's dihedral is produced by a bow string. A looped nylon string is laid around the ends of the spar (see the Eddy instructions, page 23). Finally, fit a whizzer to the head of the Janggaan, clipped to the spine. (For instructions on

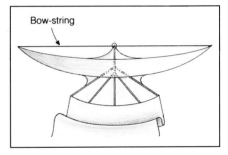

Bow-string

making the whizzer see the Wau Bulan, page 53.)

In favourable weather conditions the kite can be hand launched, but a high start launch is certainly more reliable.

sail and glue it around the frame. Cut out the sails for the head and tail, allowing 2.5 cm/1 in extra for the hem. Then cut a slit of 2.5 cm/1 in in the sail around the spars and curves. Note that at this point the frame is on the rear of the sail.

Glue the head and tail sails to the frame around the ellipse on the existing sail. I use a polystyrene ball and strips of pergamyn to decorate the head of the Janggaan. A 20 cm/ 7¾ in wide strip of paper is rolled up and cut with scissors. Slide the pergamyn strips over the tip and stick it down with sellotape.

A polystyrene ball forms the actual head of the Janggaan. The ball

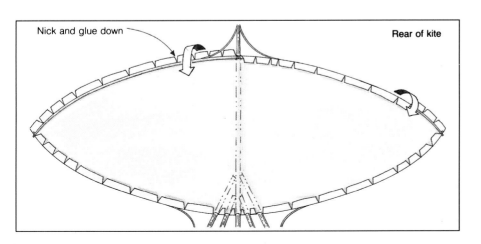

Nick and glue down

Rear of kite

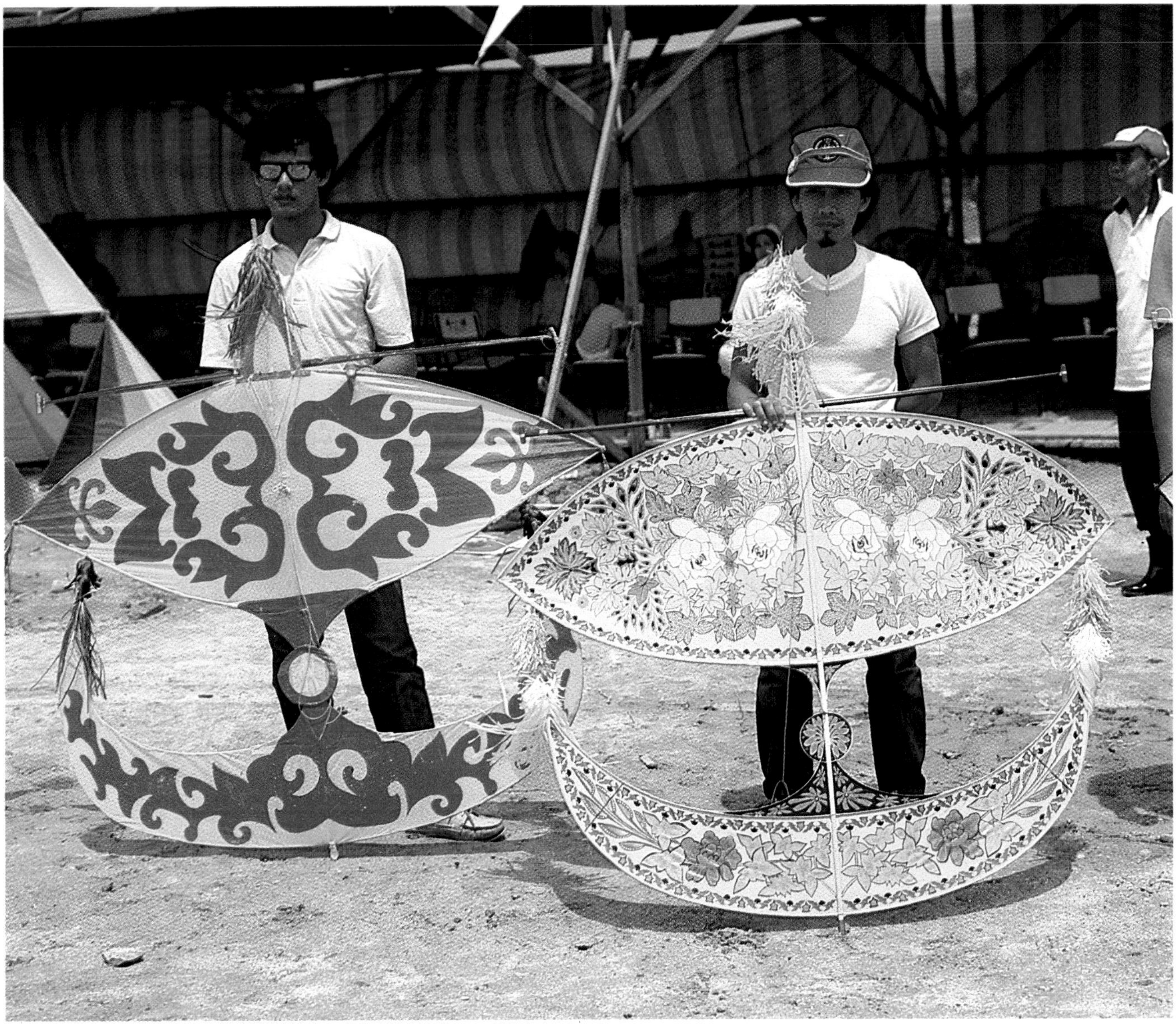

Wau Bulan

The Wau Bulan is probably the most important kite in Malaysia. On account of the crescent shape at the rear of the kite the Wau Bulan is also known as the moon kite. Although the kite's unusual form suggests that it has few positive flight qualities the opposite is, in fact, the case. The elliptical sail curves upwards in the wind and stabilises the kite. Although it flies without a tail it has a whizzer which is attached to the forward section.

Once launched the kite's flight path follows a flat figure of eight, for which it requires a large air space. However, at the Singapore kite festival the Wau Bulans are flown in a specified area to avoid collisions with other kites. The Wau Bulan is decorated at the head and sides with plenty of colourful strips of paper.

Materials:
1.5 m/1¾ yd tyvek or pergamyn
1 split bamboo rod (or cane) 132 cm/52 in long, 0.9 × 0.55 cm/⅓ × ⅕ in
2 split bamboo rods, 155 cm/61 in long, 0.9 × 0.55 cm/⅓ × ⅕ in
1 split bamboo rod, 147 cm/57¾ in long, 0.4 × 0.4 cm/⅛ × ⅛ in
1 split bamboo rod, 200 cm/78¾ in long, 0.5 × 0.4 cm/⅕ × ⅛ in
Rattan tubing
Nylon string, diam 0.1 cm/1/20 in
1 ring, diam 1.8 cm/¾ in
1 bamboo cane for the whizzer, 120 cm/47¼ in long, 1 × 0.6 cm/⅖ × ¼ in
2 pieces of tubing, interior diam 1 cm/⅖ in
Dacron ribbon, 1 cm/⅖ in wide
Fishing line

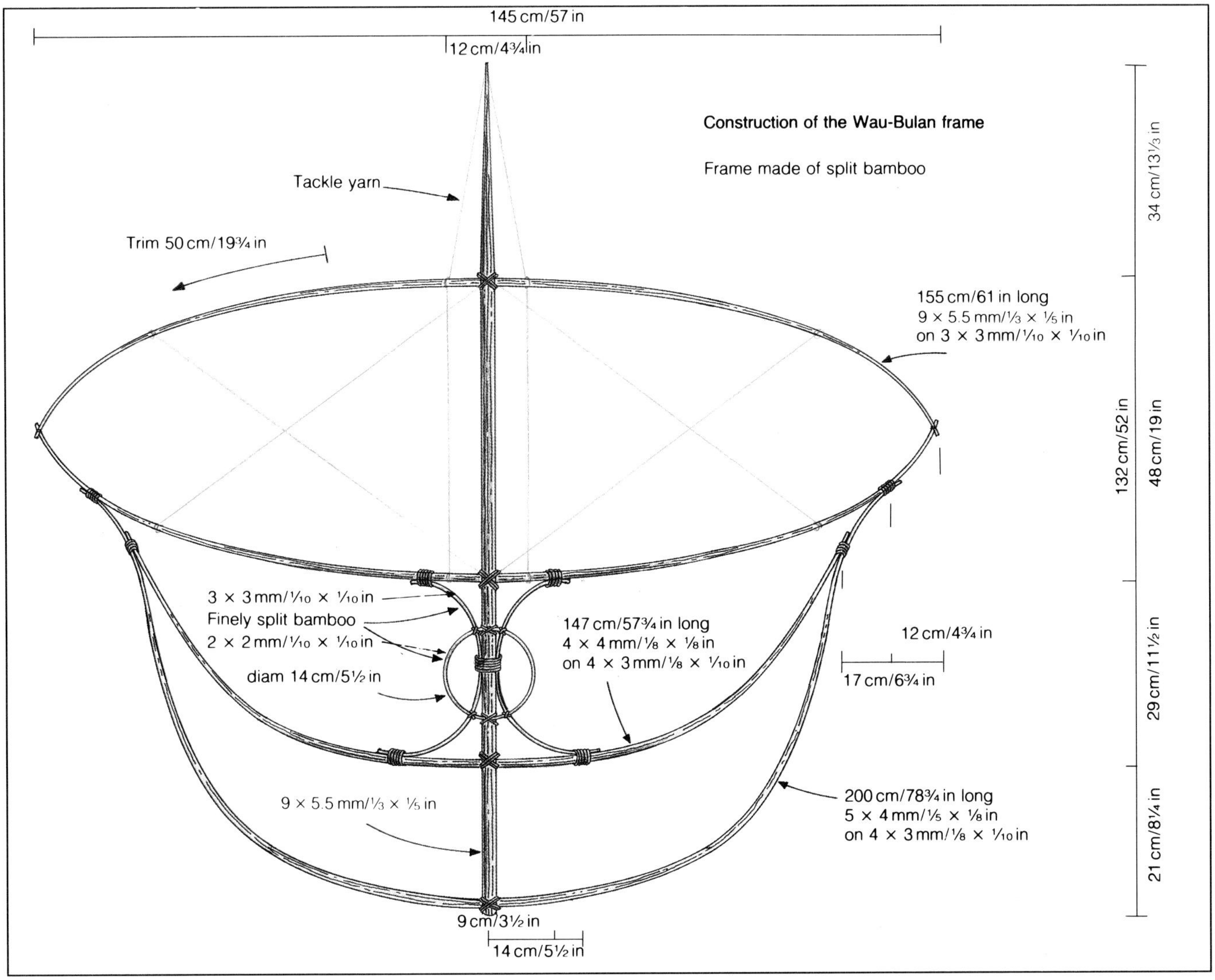

145 cm/57 in
12 cm/4¾ in
Construction of the Wau-Bulan frame
Frame made of split bamboo
Tackle yarn
Trim 50 cm/19¾ in
34 cm/13⅓ in
155 cm/61 in long
9 × 5.5 mm/⅓ × ⅕ in
on 3 × 3 mm/⅒ × ⅒ in
132 cm/52 in
48 cm/19 in
3 × 3 mm/⅒ × ⅒ in
Finely split bamboo
2 × 2 mm/⅒ × ⅒ in
diam 14 cm/5½ in
147 cm/57¾ in long
4 × 4 mm/⅛ × ⅛ in
on 4 × 3 mm/⅛ × ⅒ in
12 cm/4¾ in
17 cm/6¾ in
29 cm/11½ in
9 × 5.5 mm/⅓ × ⅕ in
200 cm/78¾ in long
5 × 4 mm/⅕ × ⅛ in
on 4 × 3 mm/⅛ × ⅒ in
21 cm/8¼ in
9 cm/3½ in
14 cm/5½ in

Instructions:

The kite's frame is made from bamboo. Essentially the whole piece can be made from one split bamboo cane 3–4 cm/1¼–1½ in thick. The central element, the ellipse, is made of two split sticks with a cross-section of 0.9 × 0.55 cm/⅓ × ⅕ in and a length of 155 cm/61 in. Trim them down towards the ends to 0.3 × 0.3 cm/⅒ × ⅒ in. If you have difficulties in keeping the split on the 155 cm/61 in cane parallel then you can use four equal pieces instead. The sticks should overlap by about 20 cm/7¾ in at the spine.

Make the 132 cm/52 in long spine from split bamboo. Fasten the two spars of the ellipse to the spine (cross-lashing, see techniques 1, page 78).

Fishing line is best for binding the sections of the frame together. Tie the ends of the two spars together. The optimum shape of the main sail is the outline of a flattened lentil. As with the spars of the ellipse, the 200 cm/78¾ in long spar of the crescent can be made in two parts. The 0.5 × 0.4 cm/⅕ × ⅛ in thick spar is trimmed down to 0.4 × 0.3 cm/⅛ × ⅒ in towards the ends. Secure the crescent shaped spar to the spine and to the ellipse (see illustration for position and form). The 147 cm/57¾ in long crescent-shaped spar is trimmed from 0.4 × 0.4 cm/⅛ × ⅛ in down to 0.4 × 0.3 cm/⅛ × ⅒ in towards the ends and secured to the spine/spar. It is up to you to decide what radius to make the curve of the crescent.

The bowed middle sections of the Wau Bulan with their small radii can be made of split bamboo or rattan. For the two semicircles I have used split bamboo sticks (0.3 × 0.3 cm/⅒ × ⅒ in) which are secured to the spines and spars.

Making the ring (14 cm/5½ in diam, made from split sticks 0.2 × 0.2 cm/⅒ × ⅒ in thick) requires a little flair. Shaping the sticks is made easier by warming them over boiling water. The elliptical section of the frame is braced with string.

The covering for the frame is cut

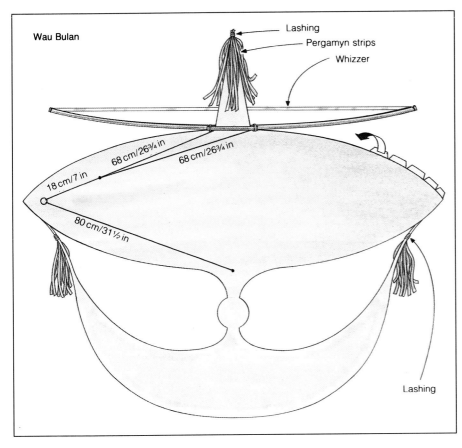

Wau Bulan

Lashing
Pergamyn strips
Whizzer
68 cm/26¾ in
68 cm/26¾ in
18 cm/7 in
80 cm/31½ in
Lashing

up a 30 cm/11¾ in wide piece of pergamyn and cut.

The paper strips are attached to the spars with fishing line or sellotape. Tie the three stringed connecting bridle to the spars. Reinforce the hole made for the rear bridle with a piece of tyvek. A 1.8 cm/¾ in ring is used for the bridle's towing point. A whizzer is an essential feature on the Wau Bulan and is made from a piece of split bamboo (1 × 0.6 cm/²⁄₅ × ¼ in). A double layer of ripstop nylon will also serve as a whizzer.

Trim the 120 cm/47¼ in long bow down to 0.6 × 0.4 cm/¼ × ⅛ in at the end. The bow is fixed to the frame with a clip device, made of a c. 16 cm/6¼ in long strip of split bamboo. One end of the clip is lashed to the bow. A movable ring secures the clip to the bow (see illustration). A 1 cm/²⁄₅ in wide strip of dacron is secured to the ends of the bow with pieces of tubing.

The kite enjoys a slight upwards curve. The bow string is secured to the tips of the ellipse (see Janggaan and Eddy). Always give the Wau Bulan a high launch. Run out at least 30 m/32¾ yd of string.

If there are strong winds the Malaysians will fly their kites at night; the increasing noise produced by the whizzers acts as a storm warning.

out of a single piece of tyvek, though the Malaysians use pergamyn. They cut decorations into the paper and glue them on in several layers, one on top of the other. This gives the sail greater solidity and an inlaid look. Lay the covering material out on an even surface. The frame will serve as a stencil and is placed on

to the tyvek with the spine downwards. Cut out the sail allowing 2.5 cm/1 in for the hem. Make 2.5 cm/1 in long slits into the material in the curved sections and glue around the frame.

The Wau Bulan is decorated with colourful strips of paper at the top and around the sides. To do this roll

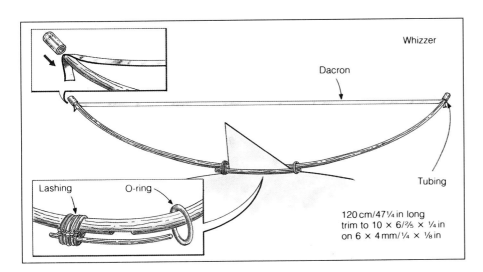

Whizzer
Dacron
Tubing
Lashing O-ring
120 cm/47¼ in long
trim to 10 × 6/²⁄₅ × ¼ in
on 6 × 4 mm/¼ × ⅛ in

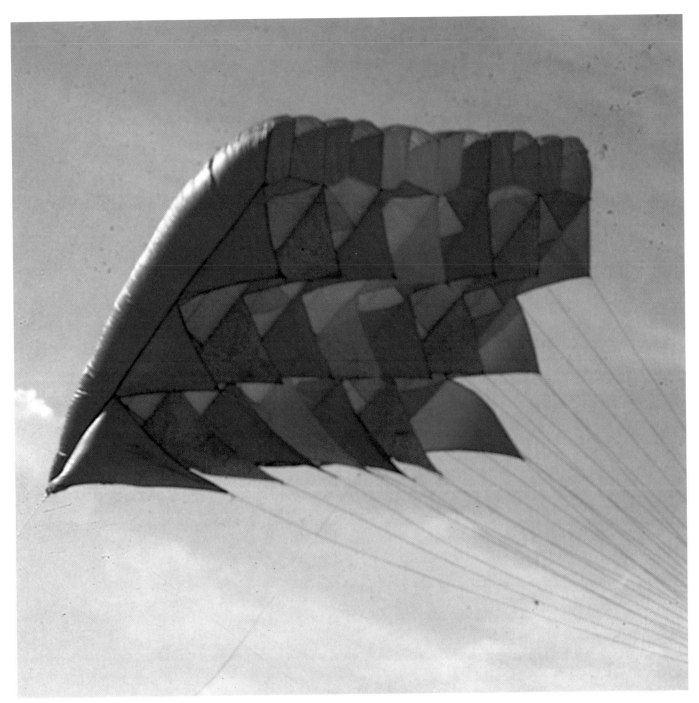

Parafoil

The parafoil is one of the most important developments in the history of kite making. Its inventor, the American D. C. Jalbert, pursued the idea that the form should follow wind flow to its logical conclusion, so creating a flexible aerofoil which, divided into cells, uses the wind pressure to retain its shape.

The enormous lift and steep angle of flight make the parafoil a real sky anchor. It has military applications, can be used for meteorological readings, and can also solve transportation problems in inaccessible areas.

Materials:
13 m²/140 ft² ripstop nylon
15 m/16½ yd dacron tape, 1 cm/⅖ in wide
Nylon string, diam 0.2 cm/¹⁄₁₀ in
1 ring, diam 3 cm/1¼ in

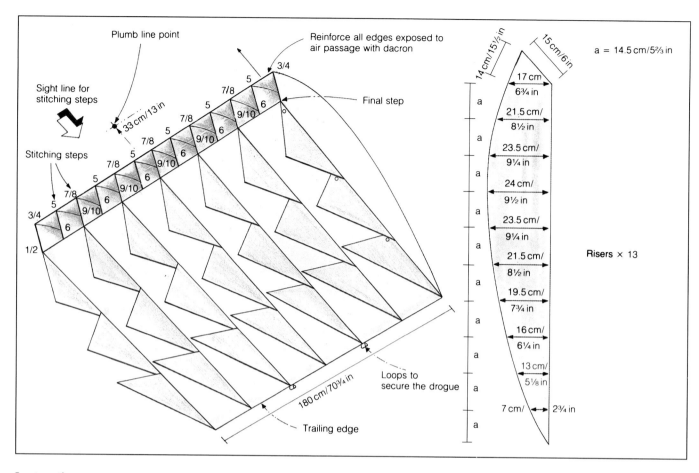

Plumb line point

Sight line for stitching steps

Reinforce all edges exposed to air passage with dacron

Final step

33 cm/13 in

Stitching steps

3/4
1/2

a = 14.5 cm/5⅔ in

14 cm/15½ in

15 cm/6 in

17 cm
6¾ in

21.5 cm/
8½ in

23.5 cm/
9¼ in

24 cm/
9½ in

23.5 cm/
9¼ in

21.5 cm/
8½ in

19.5 cm/
7¾ in

16 cm/
6¼ in

13 cm/
5⅛ in

7 cm/   2¾ in

Risers × 13

180 cm/70¾ in

Loops to secure the drogue

Trailing edge

Instructions:

If you follow the guidelines and sewing instructions exactly, constructing a parafoil will not be as difficult as it might appear. The extensive sewing work does, however, require previous experience of sewing ripstop nylon.

The measurements for this parafoil can be increased or reduced to scale. In so doing, the revised drag conditions should be borne in mind.

At average wind speeds you can reckon on 6 kg/13¼ lb drag per square metre/square yard of the parafoil's surface area.

First, cut out the risers, ventrals, faces and bottom surfaces using

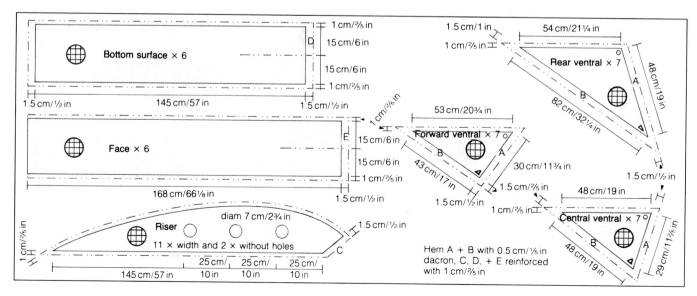

Bottom surface × 6

1 cm/⅖ in
15 cm/6 in
15 cm/6 in
1 cm/⅖ in

D

1.5 cm/½ in   145 cm/57 in   1.5 cm/½ in

Face × 6

E
15 cm/6 in
15 cm/6 in
1 cm/⅖ in

168 cm/66⅛ in   1.5 cm/½ in

Riser
diam 7 cm/2¾ in
11 × width and 2 × without holes

1 cm/⅖ in

1.5 cm/½ in

145 cm/57 in   25 cm/ 10 in   25 cm/ 10 in   25 cm/ 10 in

C

1.5 cm/1 in
1 cm/⅖ in

54 cm/21¼ in

Rear ventral × 7

48 cm/19 in
82 cm/32¼ in
B
A

1.5 cm/½ in

1 cm/⅖ in

53 cm/20¾ in

Forward ventral × 7
B
A
43 cm/17 in

30 cm/11¾ in

1.5 cm/⅖ in
1.5 cm/½ in

48 cm/19 in

1 cm/⅖ in

Central ventral × 7
B
A
48 cm/19 in
29 cm/11⅖ in

Hem A + B with 0.5 cm/⅕ in dacron, C, D, + E reinforced with 1 cm/⅖ in

56

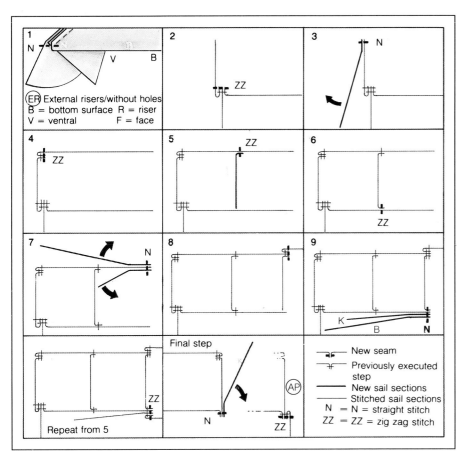

1
N · V · B
(ER) External risers/without holes
B = bottom surface   R = riser
V = ventral   F = face

2
ZZ

3
N

4
ZZ

5
ZZ

6
ZZ

7
N

8

9
K · B · N

Final step
AP

Repeat from 5

N · ZZ

New seam
Previously executed step
New sail sections
Stitched sail sections
N = N = straight stitch
ZZ = ZZ = zig zag stitch

---

cardboard stencils. That way, you can remake all or parts of the kite any time you wish.

Next, edges A, B, C, D and E are hemmed. Sew in dacron tape to strengthen the hems (see sewing techniques 2, page 77). Give added reinforcement to the ventrals by stitching dacron to their tips and add eyelets (see sewing techniques 6).

Use a soldering iron to cut 7 cm/ 2¾ in circles out of the 11 central risers. The holes help balance the pressure in the cells and should make the launch easier.

Mark the centre lines of the faces and bottom surfaces in pencil. The parafoil is sewn together from the left-hand side. Be sure to sew the seams carefully because the seams within the cells cannot be altered once they have been sewn. Securing the seams with pins or adhesive makes the sewing easier. The sectional drawing shows the sequence of stitches.

1. Sew together a bottom surface, ventral and external riser. Ensure that the ventrals' leading edges run inwards to the point of intersection.
2. The seam produced by this is sewn securely to the riser.
3. Sew a bottom surface to the external riser.
4. Sew the seam to the bottom surface with a zigzag stitch.
5. Sew a riser to the marked line of the face using a zigzag stitch.
6. Sew the riser to the marked line of the bottom surface using a zigzag stitch.
7. Sew together a fresh face piece and fresh riser to the existing bottom surface.
8. Sew the seam securely to the face piece using a zigzag stitch.
9. Sew together a riser, bottom surface, three ventrals and a fresh bottom surface.
10. Sew the seam to the bottom surface securely.

Now, repeat stitch steps 5, 6, 7, 8, 9, 10, and then 5, 6, 7, 8, 9, 10 and so on.

The final seam is on the outside (bottom surface, external riser, and ventrals). The seam is sewn secure at the ventrals. Should there be any overhanging material cut off at the trailing edge. The trailing edge is doubled over and secured with a hem.

There are two ways of bridling the parafoil:
1. To make the kite fly level – the bridle is attached as described in detail for the multiflare on page 37. The plumbline point lies 33 cm/13 in beyond the leading edge.
2. To make the kite fly curved – secure the 21 lines (all of the same length) to the ventrals (half blood knot). Draw together the lines of

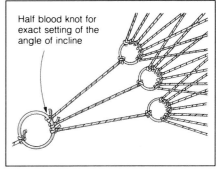

Half blood knot for exact setting of the angle of incline

the forward, central and rear ventrals and secure to a ring. Join the series of lines to a joint towing ring with a three-stringed connecting bridle.

The angle of incline is best discovered experimentally in flight. A connecting bridle should also be fitted when trying out the first method to determine the parafoil's angle of incline.

If the parafoil is unsteady in flight it is best to stabilise it with a drogue.

Wind Turbine

Kite directional stability can be influenced effectively by using tails, drogues or wind turbines. As early as the 19th century, Sir George

Nares discovered that the leverage on a wind-filled drogue is many times greater than that on a common string. A rotating drogue (wind turbine) develops additional stability. Just as with a normal tail, the longer the line of drogues the longer the lever arm, so increasing the stabilising power exerted on the kite.

Wind turbines are an attractive decoration on the kite string. At

festivals you will see marvellous wind turbines of several metres diameter, and lengths of more than 40 m/43¾ yd.

Materials:
0.45m²/4¾ ft² ripstop nylon
60 cm/23¾ in PVC tubing, diam 0.7 cm/¼ in
Nylon string, 0.1 cm/¹⁄₂₀ in
1 carabiner with swivel
1 wood dowel, diam 0.7 cm/¼ in

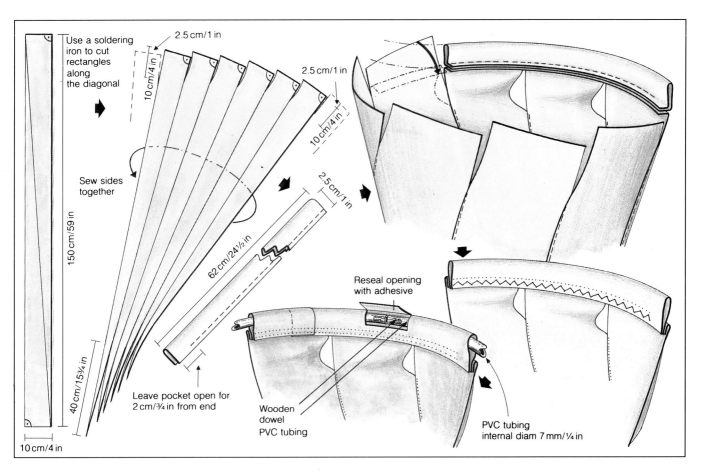

Use a soldering iron to cut rectangles along the diagonal

2.5 cm/1 in

10 cm/4 in

2.5 cm/1 in

10 cm/4 in

Sew sides together

150 cm/59 in

40 cm/15¾ in

10 cm/4 in

62 cm/24½ in

2.5 cm/1 in

Leave pocket open for 2 cm/¾ in from end

Wooden dowel
PVC tubing

Reseal opening with adhesive

PVC tubing internal diam 7 mm/¼ in

Instructions:

Use a soldering iron to cut out three rectangles with sides of 10×150 cm/ 4×59 in. Cut the rectangles along their diagonals to make six triangles. Sew together the triangles with a 2.5 cm/⅖ in displacement on each one (see illustration).

Note:
1. There should be 10 cm/4 in open on the first one and 40 cm/1⅓ ft on the last.
2. Lay all the seams in one direction.
3. Always sew a right angled section to a non-right angled section.

Once you have sewn the six sections together, sew the first and sixth section together, again with a 2.5 cm/⅖ in displacement. Turn the turbine inside out.

Cut out a thin strip of ripstop nylon, 5×62 cm/2 × 24½ in. Sew it lengthwise to form a pocket. Sew the hem of this pocket to the six edges of the triangles.

The edges are sewn on in such a way as to produce spatula-shaped openings. These should run into one another at the beginning and end of the pocket.

Sew the hem you have now made with a zigzag stitch (see illustration).

Cut a small opening in the pocket.

Cut the PVC tubing to length (according to the circumference of the turbine). A 2 cm/¾ in wood dowel connects the beginning and end of the tube. The turbine is fitted with a four stringed bridle. The 30 cm/11¾ in long lines are secured to a swivel and carabiner.

The size of the turbine can be altered by changing the measurements given to scale. If the turbine is to be fixed to the kite string there should be no knots in the string (danger of breaking) and a ring should be secured to the turbine making it slip resistant (stitch or lash it to the string). Parafoils have a high towing power so they are suited to carrying wind turbines.

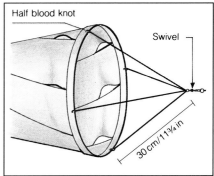

Half blood knot

Swivel

30 cm/11¾ in

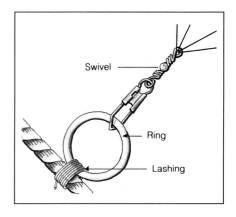

Swivel

Ring

Lashing

Box Delta

One of the great kite makers was Lawrence Hargrave. His box kite, invented in 1893, was a revolution in kite construction and became the basis of many aerodynamic experiments conducted by pioneering aviators of his time. The stabilising effect of the wings made the tail, then commonly used, superfluous.

The advantage of the box kite is that it is stable in flight even at high wind speeds. Its disadvantage is the small surface area in relation to weight. Two wings at the side of the box kite improve the ratio. The box delta, compared to its predecessor, gains a 30 per cent increase in surface area for only a 15 per cent increase in weight. The combination of effective delta wings and the stable flight of the box kite make the box delta a success. This tyvek version is particularly suitable for painting with acrylic paints and decorating with paper streamers.

Materials:
1.5 m/1¾ yd tyvek
8 pieces of dowelling, 100 cm/39⅓ in long, diam 0.6 cm/¼ in
1 piece of dowelling, 100 cm/39⅓ in long, diam 0.7 cm/¼ in
Carpet adhesive tape
Nylon string, diam 0.1 cm/1⁄20 in
1 ring, diam 1.2 cm/½ in
Synthetic tubing, 3.5 cm/1⅓ in long, internal diam 0.6 cm/¼ in
Leftover pieces of tyvek

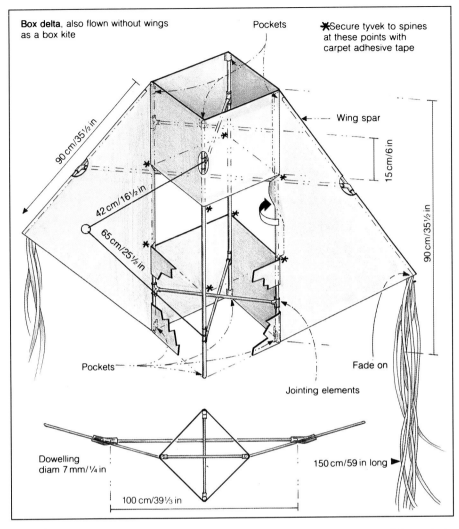

Box delta, also flown without wings as a box kite

Pockets

✳ Secure tyvek to spines at these points with carpet adhesive tape

Wing spar

90 cm/35½ in

42 cm/16½ in

65 cm/25½ in

15 cm/6 in

90 cm/35½ in

Pockets

Jointing elements

Fade on

150 cm/59 in long ▶

Dowelling diam 7 mm/¼ in

100 cm/39⅓ in

Instructions:

Begin by cutting out the two box sails. Remember to allow for the hems. Hem the vertical sides of the sails, use adhesive or machine stitch them. Mark the positions for the spine pockets at 30 cm/11¾ in intervals. Glue or sew together the two

ends on both sails keeping the seam on the inside (see illustration).

Make four pockets each for the forward and rear box sails (see gluing techniques 7 and 8). Glue or sew on the pockets at the positions marked on the sails.

Cut a 2 cm/¾ in large hole into the sails to make way for the bridle lines (for position see illustration).

Saw four spines of diam 0.6 cm/¼ in to a length of 90 cm/35½ in.

Cut out eight pieces of tubing of 0.6 cm/½ in internal diameter with a length of 3.5 cm/1⅓ in.

Cut a 2 cm/¾ in long slit down one side of each of the pieces of tubing. These pieces will form the T-joint elements for the spines and spars (see jointing techniques 10, page 78).

The jointing elements (two for each spine) are secured 15 cm/6 in from the ends of the spines with a lashing or with sellotape (see illustration for position).

Saw four spars of 0.6 cm/¼ in diameter to a length of 41 cm/16⅛ in.

Fit the four spines into the pockets of the two sails. Fit the spars into the jointing elements.

Secure the bridle to the spine, forward bridle leg 42 cm/16½ in, rear bridle leg 65 cm/25½ in (see illustration). The exact positioning of the bridle is made easier by using a ring for the towing point. Cut out two sails as shown in the sketch. Hem the trailing edge.

Saw two wing spars of 0.6 cm/¼ in diameter to a length of 90 cm/35½ in.

Make two pieces of connecting tubing, 3.5 cm/1⅓ in long and push on to the wing spars (see jointing techniques 11, page 78).

The hem (allow extra for the side pocket) is glued around the side spar. The tubing should be positioned in the semicircular opening.

Glue the two wings to the facing corners of the box kite. The 30 cm/11¾ in long middle section is glued around the spine. A piece of dowelling, 0.7 cm/2¾ in in diameter, 100 cm/39⅓ in long serves as a brace.

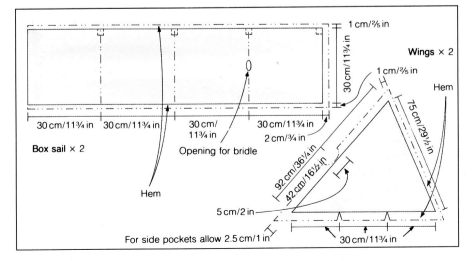

1 cm/⅖ in

30 cm/11¾ in

Wings × 2

1 cm/⅖ in

Hem

30 cm/11¾ in   30 cm/11¾ in   30 cm/11¾ in   30 cm/11¾ in

Box sail × 2

Opening for bridle

2 cm/¾ in

75 cm/29½ in

92 cm/36¼ in

42 cm/16½ in

Hem

5 cm/2 in

For side pockets allow 2.5 cm/1 in

30 cm/11¾ in

Snowflake

The snowflake is a variant on Stephen Robinson's facet kite. It is notable for its uncomplicated construction which enables it to be easily assembled in the field. And its three dimensional form produces good flight performance in light to moderate wind speeds, and has high potential for imaginative colouring, making it an extraordinary kite. However, do choose the colours carefully. Light shades in the centre (the large squares) gradually darkening towards the edge is particularly effective. In the version shown here each individual square has been divided into several colours.

Materials:
7 m²/75⅓ ft² ripstop nylon
6 pieces of dowelling, 77 cm/30⅓ in long, diam 1 cm/⅖ in
1 piece of dowelling, 155 cm/61 in long, diam 0.8 cm/⅓ in
50 cm/19¾ in synthetic tubing, diam 0.8 cm/⅓ in
20 rings, diam 1.6 cm/½ in
Nylon string, diam 0.1 cm/⅖ in
2 arrow heads

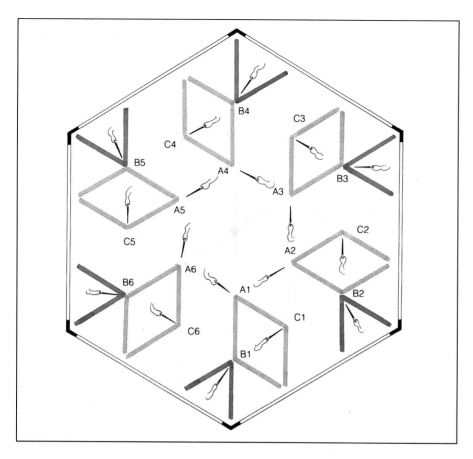

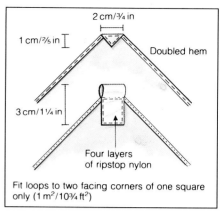

Doubled hem

Fit loops to two facing corners of one square only (1 m²/10¾ ft²)

2 cm/¾ in wide and 3 cm/1¼ in long loop which can be made of multiple layers of nylon string, webbing or seaming tape.

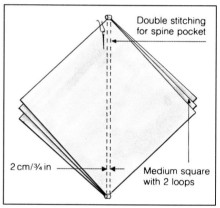

Double stitching for spine pocket

Medium square with 2 loops

Lay three large squares (1 m²/10¾ ft²) exactly on top of one another, secure with pins. Sew two diagonal hems at a 2 cm/¾ in interval to make pocket for the spine.

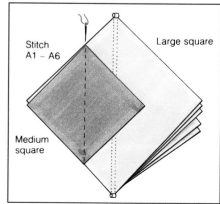

Stitch A1 – A6

Large square

Medium square

Next, sew the six A seams (A1–A6). Proceed in a clockwise fashion. The six squares (side length 66 cm/

Instructions:

The basic elements are 15 squares of light ripstop nylon (c. 32 g/m² (1⅛ oz/yd²)). Cut out three squares with sides of 1 m/1 yd, six squares with sides of 66 cm/26 in and six squares with sides of 33 cm/12 in. Co-ordinate the colours of the groups of squares. However, the colouring on individual squares can also be graduated. Rainbow coloured combinations are particularly suited for producing an attractive snowflake.

Double hem all the edges of the squares (see sewing techniques 2).

On the three large squares, you must fold over the pairs of facing corners and sew securely.

The middle square is fitted with a

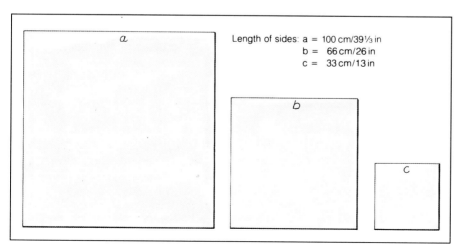

Length of sides: a = 100 cm/39⅓ in
b = 66 cm/26 in
c = 33 cm/13 in

26 in) must be laid precisely into the corners of the large squares and pinned secure. The squares must always be stitched on the same side of the corner.

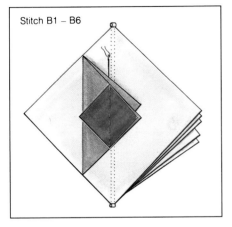

Stitch B1 – B6

The six small squares (side length 33 cm/13 in) are laid precisely into a corner of the six medium squares and pinned securely. Ensure that the small squares are always sewn on to the same sails and side of the medium squares (seam B1–B6).

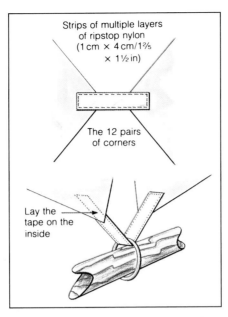

Strips of multiple layers of ripstop nylon (1 cm × 4 cm/1²⁄₅ × 1½ in)

The 12 pairs of corners

Lay the tape on the inside

These strips connect 12 corner pairs. The illustration details the pairings.

Stitch the strips to the corners from the inside. Secure a ring to each of the strips. The dowelling will later be passed through these rings.

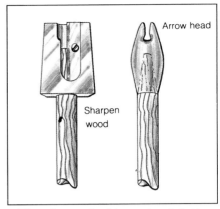

Arrow head

Sharpen wood

The pieces of tubing act as jointing elements for the frame structure. Cut the spine to the required length. It should stick out about 4 cm/1½ in beyond the pocket.

Saw the ends, 0.5 cm/¹⁄₅ in down and 0.2 cm/¹⁄₁₀ in across and then dip them in wood adhesive. Once this has dried they will have greater rigidity. A more elegant solution is to put a notched arrow head on to the sharpened end of the dowelling. Having positioned the middle spar in the pocket, secure a ring to each of

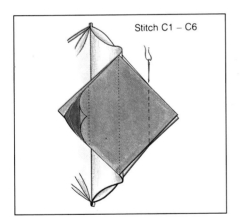

Stitch C1 – C6

Lay the corner of the medium square on the corner of the large square, pin secure and stitch. Sew seam C six times (C1–C6). In order to achieve perfect tensioning on the snowflake later, lay the sections precisely on top of one another and seam.

Make 12 strips of multi-layered ripstop nylon (1 × 4 cm/²⁄₅ × 1½ in).

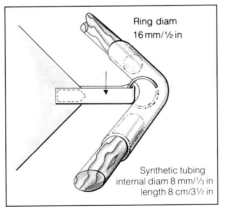

Ring diam 16 mm/½ in

Synthetic tubing internal diam 8 mm/¹⁄₃ in length 8 cm/3¹⁄₇ in

The remaining six sections are fitted with loops of multi-layered ripstop nylon.

Cut out six pieces of 8 cm/3¹⁄₈ in long tubing. Punch a hole into the middle of each with punching tongs.

Pass a ring through the hole and loop.

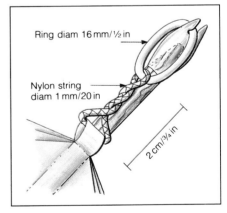

Ring diam 16 mm/½ in

Nylon string diam 1 mm/20 in

2 cm/¾ in

the sail loops with 2 cm/¾ in of string. The middle spar pockets are braced tautly, though the tension can be adjusted later by tightening the string. Cut the rods for the frame structure to length and push into the loops. The sail must be tautly braced. The bridle is secured to one tip and two corners of the frame (see photo page 63). The forward bridle leg is 127 cm/50 in, the rear 130 cm/51¹⁄₈ in.

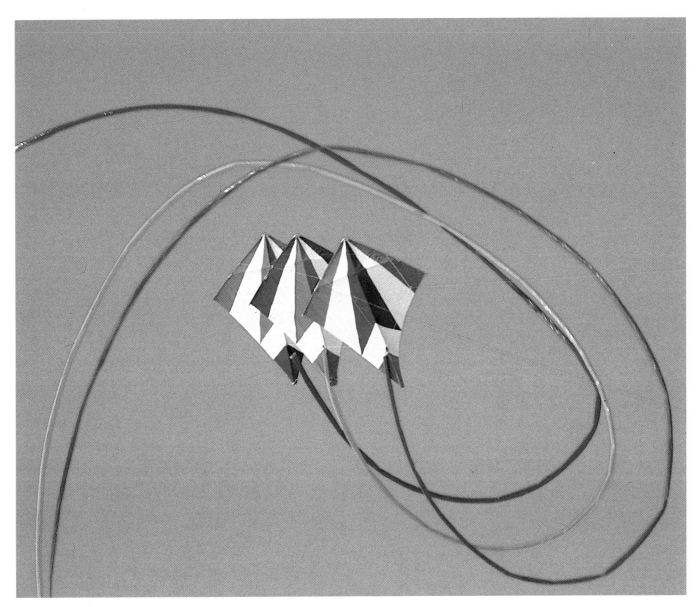

Peter Powell

Steerable kite flying is a sport that requires skill, good reactions, and sometimes strength. From the mid-1970s, when the Englishman Peter Powell first introduced the kite named after him, it began winning prizes, gaining in popularity year by year.

The Peter Powell steerable (sometimes called dirigible) kite offers precision stunt flying. Its fibre glass frame (similar to that of a Rogallo kite) and ripstop nylon covering allow it to be used in a wide range of wind speeds. A characteristic feature of the Peter Powell is its *c.* 20 m/21¾ yd long tubular tail, which copies the kite's figures like a skywriter. As with all steerable kites, the Peter Powell can be flown in trains, though increasing the number of kites can increase the drag to the point where a handler is pulled along the ground for metres.

Materials:

1.7 m/1¾ yd ripstop nylon
1 fibre glass rod, 350 cm/137¾ in
   long, diam 0.6 cm/¼ in
High-pressure tubing, 15 cm/6 in
   long, diam 0.6 cm/¼ in
T-joint element, or piece of rigid
   synthetic
7 × 2.1 cm/2¾ × ¾ in self-adhesive
   nylon
Dacron strips
Nylon string, diam 0.1 cm/¹⁄₂₀ in
2 rings, diam 1.6 cm/½ in
16 m/17½ yd PVC tubular tail

Instructions:

To make the sail for a Peter Powell kite you should use medium grade ripstop nylon (*c.* 50 g/m² [1¾ oz/ yd²]). Use a corrugated board stencil which will allow you to reproduce

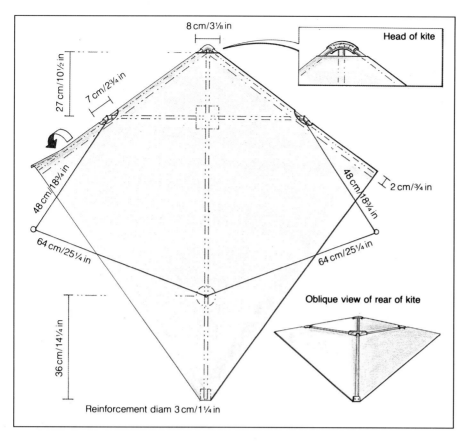

8 cm/3⅛ in

Head of kite

27 cm/10½ in

7 cm/2¾ in

48 cm/18¾ in

48 cm/18¾ in

2 cm/¾ in

64 cm/25¼ in

64 cm/25¼ in

36 cm/14¼ in

Oblique view of rear of kite

Reinforcement diam 3 cm/1¼ in

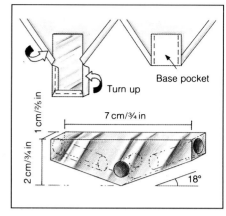

Head of kite

Turn up

Base pocket

1 cm/⅖ in

7 cm/¾ in

2 cm/¾ in

18°

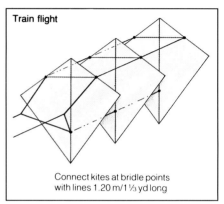

Train flight

Connect kites at bridle points
with lines 1.20 m/1⅓ yd long

the sail at any time. Do not forget to allow for the hems (see illustration).

You need to stick two pieces of self-adhesive nylon reinforcement (5 × 10 cm/2 × 4 in) to the sail in the positions as illustrated.

A 2 × 5 cm/¾ × 2 in dacron strip is sewn to the base pocket as shown. A triple layer of self-adhesive nylon will fulfil the same purpose.

Give all the edges of the sail a 0.5 cm/⅕ in hem. Cut the base

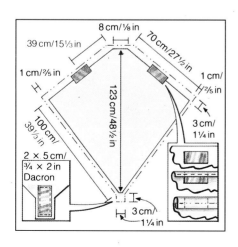

8 cm/⅛ in

39 cm/15⅓ in

70 cm/27½ in

1 cm/⅖ in

1 cm/⅖ in

123 cm/48½ in

100 cm/39⅓ in

3 cm/1¼ in

2 × 5 cm/¾ × 2 in Dacron

3 cm/1¼ in

pocket at the side (with a soldering iron) and hem likewise. Remember that the pockets and seams are on the back of the sail. Fold up the base pocket and sew on securely. Next, sew on the 2 cm/¾ in wide pockets for the wing spars. The pockets must be at least large enough to accommodate a 0.6 cm/¼ in fibre glass rod.

Use a soldering iron to cut out two semicircular openings in the pockets (see illustration for position). Make two 4 cm/1½ in tubing pieces for the side spars, and one 7 cm/2¾ in tubing piece for the head (see jointing techniques 12 and 13). The X-centre joint is available from any kite store. If you cannot buy one then make it yourself from a piece of rigid synthetic (see illustration). The rods of the kite should be matched to the sail. Insert the side spars into the pockets provided and then push the connecting tubes over the spars at the semicircular opening points. Only when you have adjusted the side spars to tubing at the head

should you cut them to their final length. The X-joint is pushed on to the 0.6 cm/¼ in fibre glass middle spar and the spar fitted in.

The two 0.6 cm/¼ in fibre glass spars should be fitted in such a way as to leave the sail braced tautly by the frame. The jointing elements should be secured against slipping with sellotape. The double bridle is secured to the tubing pieces and spine. Put self-adhesive nylon reinforcements on the rear bridle fixing point, and the cross point of the frame on the back of the sail. The tubular tail is secured to the rear bridle point on the front of the sail with a carabiner hook.

Vector

In recent years a whole series of new steerable kites have been developed in the USA. The hyperkite, sky-nasaur and Hawaiian are but a few examples. Since the majority of these new steerables are based on Rogallo's flexible surface principle, some of them (also known as stunters) can reach speeds of 100 kmph/ 62⅛ mph. However, when flying this fast the trailing edges can begin

to flutter, slowing down the flight.

In this version the fluttering is reduced to a minimum by modifying the trailing edge. The kite is distinguished by precise flight manoeuvres, high speeds and its ability to fly tight circles.

Materials:
2.5 m/2¾ yd ripstop nylon
Carbon fibre rods, 550 cm/216½ in long, diam 0.8 cm/⅓ in
2 pieces of dowelling, 118 cm/46½ in long, diam 0.7 cm/¼ in
High-pressure tubing, 30 cm/11¾ in long, diam 0.8 cm/⅓ in

High-pressure tubing, 4.5 cm/1¾ in long, diam 1.3 cm/½ in
High-pressure tubing, 24 cm/9½ in long, diam 1 cm/⅖ in
Seaming tape, 13 m/14¼ yd, 2 cm/ ¾ in wide
Webbing, 35 cm/13¾ in, 4 cm/1½ in wide
Fibre glass sellotape
Nylon string, diam 2.5 mm/¹⁄₁₀ in
2 rings, diam 3 cm/1¼ in
5 rings, diam 1.6 cm/½ in
Self-adhesive nylon
5 arrow nocks

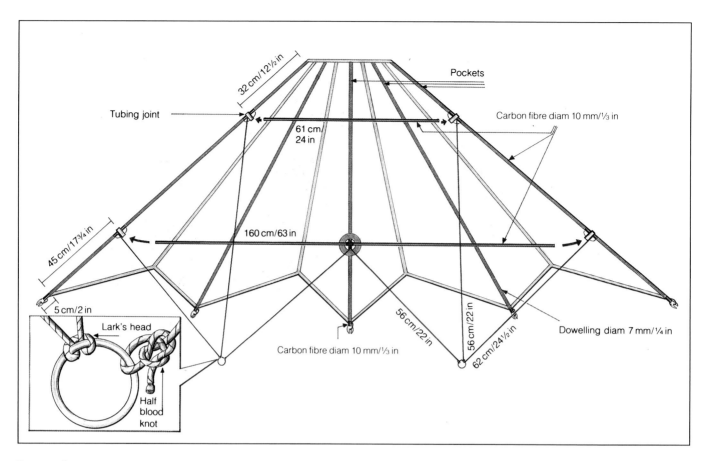

Instructions:

The sail of the steerable vector kite shown here consists of five sections which are sewn together. This combination of colours illustrate one way of decorating it.

Cut out the corrugated board stencils for the sail sections (not forgetting to allow for the hems).

Then sew together the sections using a lap seam (see sewing techniques 1). Stick four self-adhesive nylon reinforcement sections (2.5 × 12 cm/1 × 4¾ in) and a circle with a 7 cm/2¾ in circumference on to the edges of the sails and on to the sail at the rear cross point of the frame.

Now the sail is sewn right the

way round, with the reinforcement sections under the seam (see illustration). Next, the trailing edge is strengthened with a strip of black seaming tape. The seaming tape is sewn on to the seam of the sail with a double row of stitches (see illustration). Do not cut the tape at the corners, sew continuously.

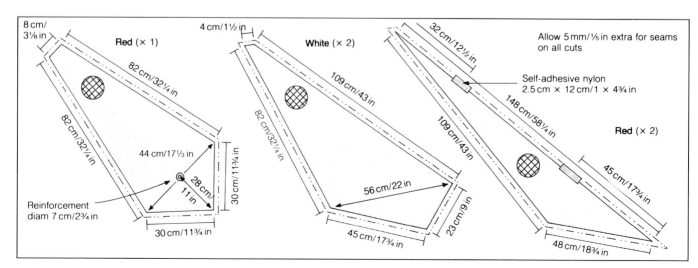

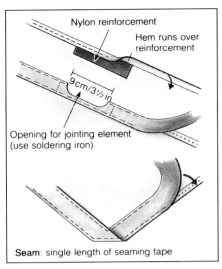

Nylon reinforcement

Hem runs over reinforcement

9 cm/3½ in

Opening for jointing element (use soldering iron)

Seam: single length of seaming tape

Sew black seaming tape along the sail's red and white overlaps. Cut the ends of the seaming tape with a soldering iron (to seal).

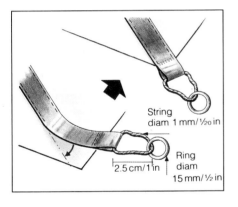

String diam 1 mm/1/20 in

2.5 cm/1 in

Ring diam 15 mm/½ in

Sew the 16 mm/½ in wide seaming tape pockets shown in the sketch on to the sail. At the rear end the tape is folded into a loop before being stitched to the sail. The loop should stick out about 1cm/⅓ in

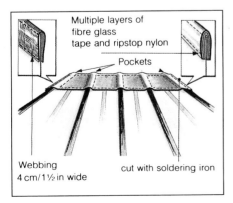

Multiple layers of fibre glass tape and ripstop nylon

Pockets

Webbing 4 cm/1½ in wide

cut with soldering iron

over the trailing edge (see illustration). Secure a 1.6 cm/½ in ring to each of these loops with string 2.5 cm/1 in from the edge.

The forward tip of the sail needs to be strongly reinforced. There are two ways of doing this.

1. Stick several layers of fibre glass reinforced film over the forward edge. A hemmed strip of ripstop nylon is stitched on to this as the final layer (see illustration).
2. A 4 cm/1½ in wide strip of webbing (as used in car safety belts) is wrapped around the edge and sewn, as in the illustration.

In both cases the ends should be sealed with a soldering iron. Use a soldering iron to cut out 9 cm/3½ in long semicircular openings in the wing edges (two on each side as illustrated). After cutting out, the outer seam must be restitched around the openings.

The side spars are made from two carbon fibre parts, each joined together with a jointing element. The carbon fibre parts are available from kite stores (see jointing techniques 8, page 78).

Four high-pressure tubes make up the jointing elements for the side and cross spars. Insert the side spars into the pockets. Push the pieces of tubing over the spars in the semicircular openings (see jointing techniques 12, page 78).

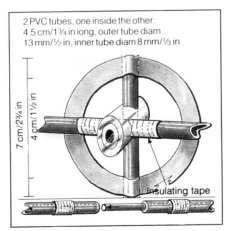

2 PVC tubes, one inside the other: 4.5 cm/1¾ in long, outer tube diam 13 mm/½ in, inner tube diam 8 mm/⅓ in

7 cm/2¾ in

4 cm/1½ in

Insulating tape

Push the two pieces of 0.7 cm/ ¼ in diameter dowelling into the pockets. Both the side spars

and dowelling should jut out approximately 5 cm/2 in from the pockets.

The T-joint that connects the middle spar and the longer rear cross spar is made from two overlapping sections of tubing (see jointing techniques 7, page 78). This cross joint is then given two drill holes set at 90° to each other for the spine and spar. Use a soldering iron to cut a 4 cm/1½ in large hole into the sail reinforcement at the cross point.

Push the spine into the pocket. The tubing joint is in the semicircular opening. Cut the spine to length.

Nick the spars at the ends to about 0.5 cm/⅕ in down. The sail should be

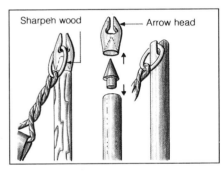

Sharpen wood

Arrow head

tautly braced. The tension can be regulated by adjusting the string between the pocket and ring (see illustration). A more elegant method is to make an arrow nock tensioner. An aluminium tip secures the arrow nock to the carbon fibre rod. The dowelling is sharpened to hold the arrow nock (see illustration).

The rear spar is made from two carbon fibre rods. The jointing piece is at the cross point (see illustration).

Saw the rear and forward spars to lengths of 160/61 cm (63/24 in) and fit into the tubing joints.

Take the bridle lengths from the sketch. The lines meet in a 3 cm/ 1¼ in ring.

Note: the bridle lines of a side spar are continuous and are connected to the ring with a loop. This allows the kite's angle of incline to be adjusted without difficulty.

Why Kites Fly

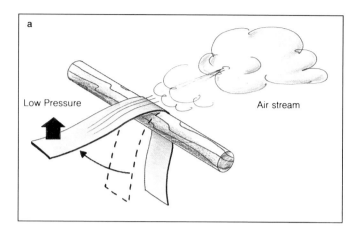

The first kites were constructed some 2,000 years ago, since when many inventors have investigated the theory of kite flying. A considerable contribution was made by the Swiss mathematician Daniel Bernoulli (1700–1782), whose theorem states that the pressure of liquids and gases diminishes with increasing velocities.

This theorem is easily proven by gently curving a *c.* 15 cm/6 in strip of paper and folding it at one end in such a way that it will hang over a pencil. Now blow over the curved side. The higher velocity on the upper side of the paper produces negative pressure on this side which forces the paper upwards (see illustration 'a'). With conventional kites which do not have a curved profile – and that is the majority of them – the uplift is produced by the air pressure at the front of the kite. The degree of this pressure depends on the angle of the kite surface. If the angle of attack is too slight (*c.* 8°) the kite's air resistance and also the pressure on the trailing edge is low. The low pressure on the rear side produces the kite's lift (see illustration 'b').

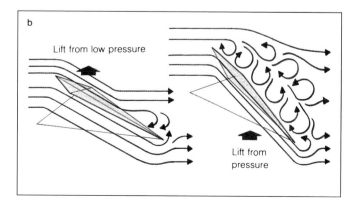

Increasing the angle of attack increases the kite's air resistance, but the air stream over the rear side is deflected producing turbulence. As a result the low pressure fades.

The pressure on the kite's forward side and the resistance of the string prevent it from sagging. Kites do indeed fly at a high angle to the wind. Experts speak of an exaggerated flight position (see illustration 'c').

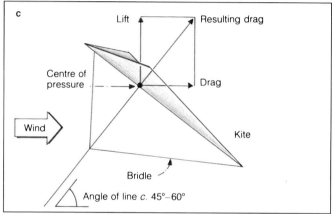

However, the turbulent air stream on the rear side does not greatly assist lift.

At a string angle of 45°–60° air resistance and lift are at a good ratio enabling the kite to take up a stable flight position. The prerequisite for this is that the lift is great enough to support the weight of the kite at an appropriate height. The exceptions are kites with risers. For example, the curved rear side of a parafoil allows it to fly at a low angle of attack.

Parafoils receive their lift from the low pressure produced on the rear side of the kite. The low angle of attack allows the parafoil to fly at an efficient string angle (*c.* 70°). However, even in normal kites the surfaces are never entirely flat. The wind pressure forces the kite sail between the spars, curved surfaces are formed and the wind is forced over the rear side of the kite.

Stability

The stability of a kite depends on several factors, including the setting of the bridle, the form, keels, and tail.

Bridle setting — in general, an imaginary extension of the towing line would point to the kite's centre of pressure (balance of the surfaces facing the wind). I have taken the bridle lengths in the instructions from my own experience in the field. If you vary the measurements of your kites then you may have to adjust the bridles. A ring at the bridle's towing point facilitates the adjustment of the angle of attack (see illustration 'd').

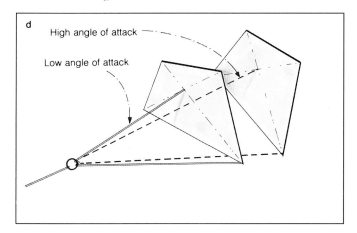

The form – dihedrals are stabilised by the self-compensating pressure on the sides. A roll to one side automatically causes higher air resistance on the other and the kite returns to position (see illustration 'e').

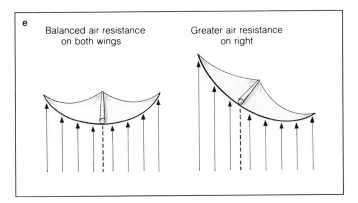

Winged kites, such as the box kite, maintain their stability through their sails which are set in the direction of the wind. Because of the stabilising effect of the wings, celled kites are able to fly stably even in gusty conditions. Box kites can be flown with the flat side to the wind enabling you to differentiate between lift and

stabilising surfaces. If the kite flies with one edge to the wind then all surfaces function as lift and stabilising surfaces (see illustration 'f').

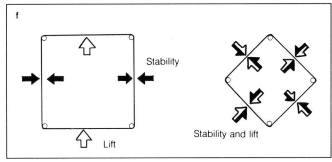

Keels – keels can be fitted to the forward or rear side of the kite. They always show the wind direction and prevent the kite from rolling to one side.

Tails – it is not the weight of drogues and tails that contributes to kite stability but their drag on the rear edge.

A selection of drogues and tails

Steerable or Stunt Kites

Steerable kites have a long history, the earliest recording being in 1861 when a Captain Nares used one to rescue shipwreck victims. His plane angled kite was flown with a second line which was secured to the base of the kite. When this line was pulled it altered the kite's angle of incline to such a degree that the kite landed setting down the shipwreck victim. If the wind was blowing out to sea the steering line was secured to one side of the kite. By pulling on this line the kite would fly sideways towards land. Giving a firmer pull caused the kite to touch down. Even today there are steerable kites very similar to Nares'.

All steerable kites are steered in the same way. The two steering lines are connected to the left and right sides of the kite by a bridle. To steer the kite, one of the lines is either pulled in or let out, altering the centre of pressure to such an extent that it begins to roll to one side. Exaggerated pulling or letting on the line produces circular movements.

In high wind speeds steerable kites respond extremely accurately to these steering manoeuvres. Skilled pilots can steer their kites horizontally, just above the ground, or on to specific targets. Steerable kites should be flown with lines between 30 m/32¾ yd and 50 m/54¾ yd long. The choice of the right string is decisive for good flight performance.

To make the kite fly perfectly, even if the string is twisted in several places, its surface must be as smooth as possible. By steering in the opposite direction the knots will quickly unravel. Even more important is the tensile strength of the string. Perfect steering manoeuvres are only possible if the kite's reaction to the manoeuvre is not delayed by the string stretching.

Trevira strings have proven to be the best because they have a smooth surface and a high tensile strength. However, steerable kite specialists use lines made from aramid, such as kevlar, twaron or herculine. These carbon fibre strings are characterised by their comparatively narrow cross section for equal ultimate strength. This reduces the air resistance on the string enabling the kite to fly faster.

A steerable kite always achieves its highest speed against the wind near ground level where its air resistance is greatest. The higher the kite flies against the wind the lower its speed and drag. At its highest point the kite will stand still.

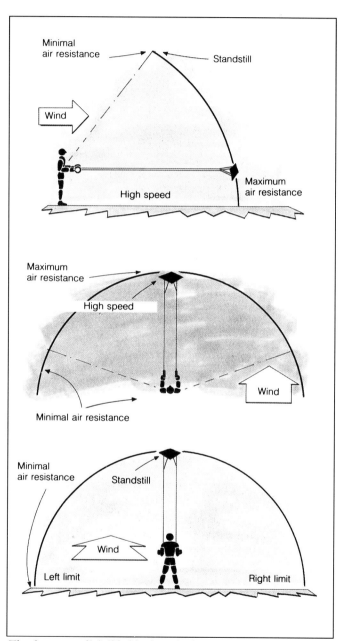

The drag on a dirigible kite is at its lowest when it has reached its zenith. The higher the kite climbs the lower its speed and, eventually, it comes to a complete standstill. If the kite is manoeuvred vertically downwards from this position its air resistance will steadily increase. This leads to increases in drag and speed. Dirigible kites can be steered up to a certain angle against the wind (comparable with the tacking of a sail boat).

Flying Steerable Kites

Skilled steerable kite pilots can launch their kites without help. Lay out two equal lines of about 50 m/ 54¾ yd (to produce perfect manoeuvres the lines must be exactly the same length). You should be able to vary the length of the lines in the light of local conditions. To facilitate the launch and flight the string should be attached to a reel. You will find it an enormous benefit if you drill four holes into the sides of the reel. By means of a fibre glass plug secured firmly in the holes the exact string length can be measured (see illustration).

Having laid out the lines, secure the reels in the ground with a wooden pole. Steerable kites should always be secured to the line with a strong carabiner and swivel (see illustration). The kite must be set up directly into the wind. Kites with a flat rear edge, such as the vector, are set up vertically to the wind. Kites such as the Peter Powell are positioned on one spar. Compensatory

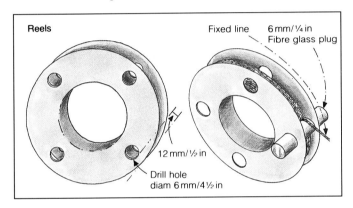

Reels   Fixed line   6 mm/¼ in
Fibre glass plug
12 mm/½ in
Drill hole
diam 6 mm/4½ in

line pressure prevents the kite from falling over. Launch the kite by pulling on both steering lines at the same time.

It is important to choose open terrain when flying a steerable kite. A short tug is all that is needed to set the kite climbing upwards (this launch procedure also applies to kite trains).

Given equal drag on the steering lines a steerable kite will always fly in the same direction as the point

indicates. This means that even for a horizontal flight both lines must be pulled evenly.

There are two ways of flying steerable kites:
1. Direct control of the lines by hand or loops.
2. Using a steering rod to transfer the hand movements to the lines.

A greater feel for the movement, and with it a more exact execution of the figures, is achieved by direct hand control. Steering rods are suited to steerable kites with greater drag or larger trains. Sometimes the drag is so strong that pilots tie themselves to cars or trees to avoid being pulled along the ground.

The Kite Society of Great Britain held its first stunt kite flying championships in 1988 at York. The figures below show the participants' compulsory programme in a German competition. They were judged on symmetry and accuracy in performing the figures and, in addition, had to perform a freestyle programme lasting one minute.

To avoid accidents you should always use perfect equipment when flying your kite. And remember, flying the kite near ground level can frighten people and animals.

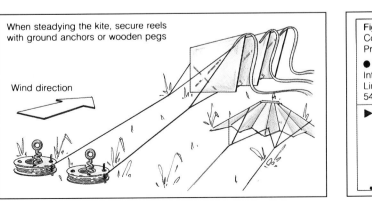

When steadying the kite, secure reels with ground anchors or wooden pegs

Wind direction

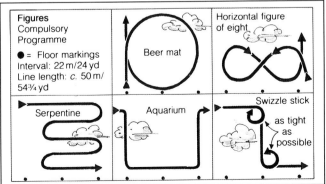

Figures
Compulsory
Programme

● = Floor markings
Interval: 22 m/24 yd
Line length: c. 50 m/ 54¾ yd

Beer mat

Horizontal figure of eight

Serpentine

Aquarium

Swizzle stick
as tight as possible

Flying Technique

There is nothing more important for the kite maker than the first test flights with a recently finished kite. Often poor weather conditions or lack of wind will prevent the first launch, making the wait for advantageous conditions a test of patience.

Optimum wind speeds for a successful launch are between 15 and 30 kmph/9⅓ and 18¾ mph, though kites such as the flare or delta will fly in even weaker winds. Box and steerable kites can take wind speeds of 50 kmph/31 mph and over.

Choose open terrain for the launch. Avoid the lee side (the side away from the wind) of tall buildings and trees because there will be turbulence which will make the launch more difficult. Tall chimneys and pylons in particular should be avoided. The beach is the best launch site because there will be hardly any difficulty in hand launching the kite into a wind blowing inland from the sea. However, do always take other people's safety into account when launching a kite – a crowded beach is definitely to be avoided because a reel sent flying along the ground can cause serious injuries.

Where winds are blowing from land to sea you should note how high the kite is flying. Many a kite has been lost when the line has broken far out over the sea freeing the kite to disappear beneath the waves. You should not let the line run out freely from the reel on a hand launch. Let the kite continue to gain height by short checks on the line.

If the wind conditions near ground level are inadequate, or if ground turbulence is causing problems, then you will need to make a high start launch. This involves laying out 30 m/100 yd of line. An assistant should hold the kite against the wind and, after a few short tugs on the line, you will raise the kite. Do not set off on a long run against the wind holding the line, nor should you try a launch if the wind is too weak.

Bridle Settings – Problems and Remedies

1. If the kite will not rise – shorten the forward bridle leg.
2. If the kite is too upright and flies unevenly – shorten the rear bridle leg or add a tail.
3. If the kite flies off to one side – either the kite is set too hard against the wind, so shorten the upper bridle leg slightly; or the right and left bridle legs are of unequal lengths.

Team Kite Flying

When flying kite trains or the larger kites you need team work. On Bali, kites up to 10 m/36 yd tall are flown by teams of 20 people. This makes co-ordinated action and understanding an absolute must. It is important that an experienced kite pilot gives the orders. When flying the large Rokkaku fighting kites synchronised movements are essential. For this reason in Japanese kiting competitions a drum gives the beat telling the participants when to pull or relax the line. Remember to wear gloves to prevent cut hands.

Reels
The everyday piece of wood around which the string is wound in a figure of eight is still in use. You can pull in the kite quickly even from great heights using the H or ring reels. However, the reels must be strongly built to withstand the increased drag when pulling in the kite.

When making a reel you should bear in mind the diameter of the hub. The line can be wound quickly around a hub with a large diameter, but it requires greater strength to reel it in. A more advanced reel is one built around a bicycle hub. Such reels are handy and run easily.

Ground Anchor
If there is no other option the kite can be anchored to the ground. Where there is considerable drag use two anchors twisted crosswise.

Sewing and glueing techniques

1 Lap seam

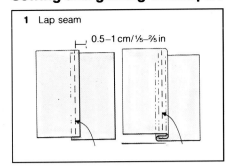

0.5–1 cm/⅕–⅖ in

2 Hemming with dacron

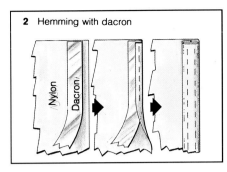

Nylon   Dacron

3 Stitching seaming tape

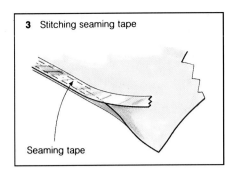

Seaming tape

4 Webbing loop

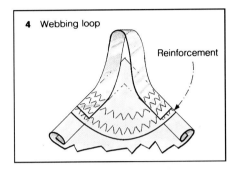

Reinforcement

5

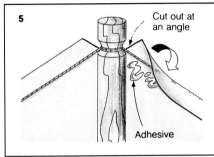

Cut out at an angle

Adhesive

6

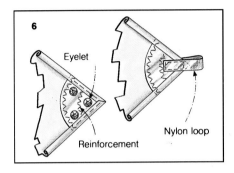

Eyelet

Nylon loop

Reinforcement

7 Box delta

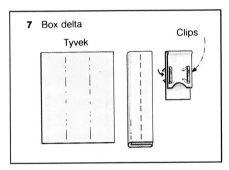

Tyvek   Clips

8 Box delta

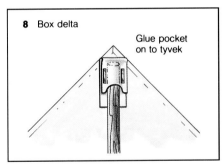

Glue pocket on to tyvek

9 Pocket made of multiple layers of nylon, dacron or webbing

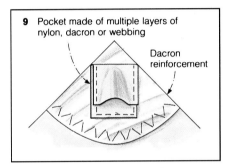

Dacron reinforcement

10

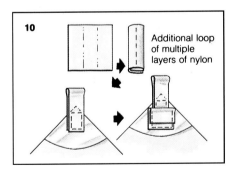

Additional loop of multiple layers of nylon

11 Pocket for middle spar

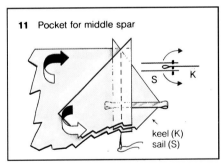

S   K

keel (K)
sail (S)

12 Pocket for middle spar

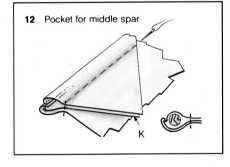

K

13 Pocket for middle spar Flaero train and delta train

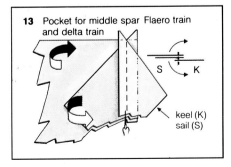

S   K

keel (K)
sail (S)

14 Pocket for middle spar Flaero train and delta train

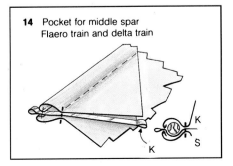

K
S
K

15 Pocket with multiple layer of nylon strips for bracing a spar

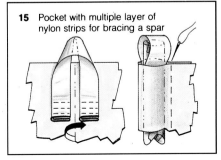

Jointing techniques

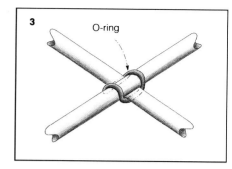

1 Cross lashing

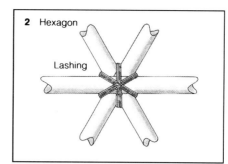

2 Hexagon

Lashing

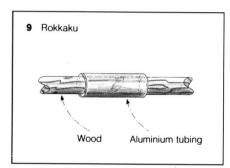

3 O-ring

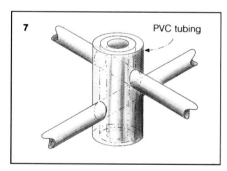

4 O-ring or elastic band — Aluminium tubing

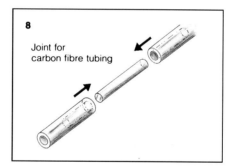

5 Lashing with fishing line

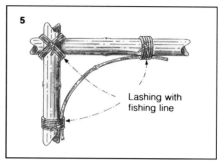

6 Synthetic tubing

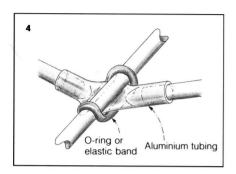

7 PVC tubing

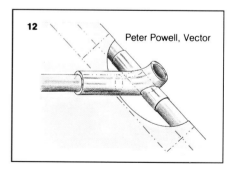

8 Joint for carbon fibre tubing

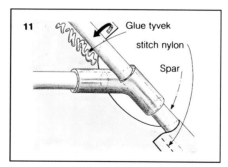

9 Rokkaku

Wood   Aluminium tubing

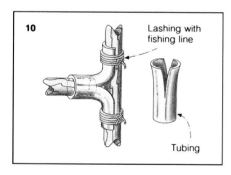

10 Lashing with fishing line

Tubing

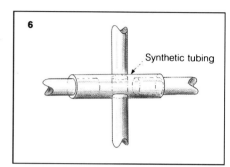

11 Glue tyvek

stitch nylon

Spar

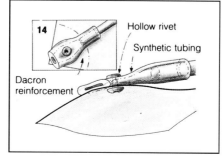

12 Peter Powell, Vector

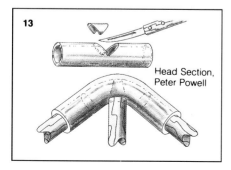

13 Head Section, Peter Powell

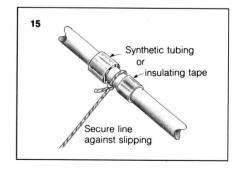

14 Hollow rivet

Synthetic tubing

Dacron reinforcement

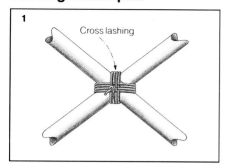

15 Synthetic tubing or insulating tape

Secure line against slipping

Knots

Round turn with 2 half hitches I
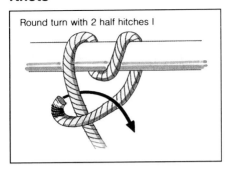

Round turn with 2 half hitches II
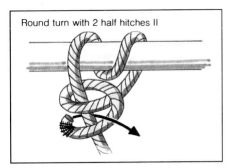

Figure of eight
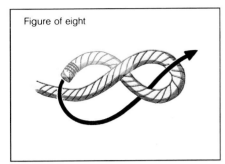

Half blood knot I
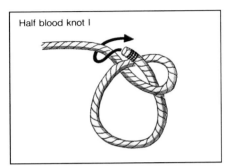

Half blood knot II
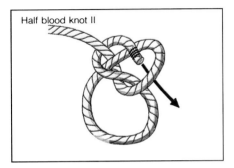

Lark's head hitch
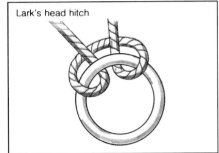

Rolling hitch I
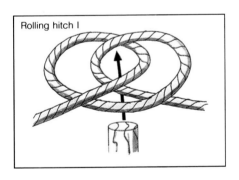

Rolling hitch II
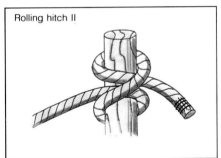

Rolling hitch on a rail
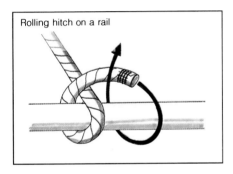

Reef knot I

Reef knot II
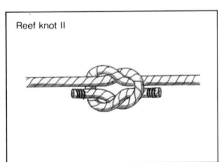

Double sheet bend I
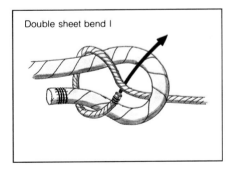

Double sheet bend II
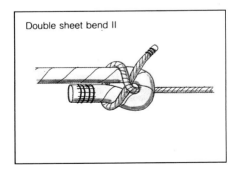

Toggle hitch I
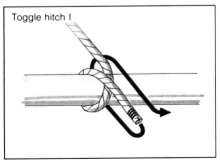

Toggle hitch II
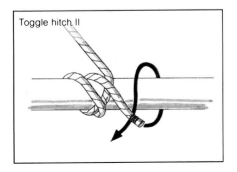

Index